Instant Pot Pressure Cooker Cookbook

550 Fresh & Foolproof Instant Pot Recipes Made for Everyday Cooking & Your Instant Pot

BY

Michael Francis

ISBN: 978-1-952504-56-3

COPYRIGHT © 2020 by Michael Francis

All rights reserved. This book is copyright protected and it's for personal use only. Without the prior written permission of the publisher, no part of this publication should be reproduced, distributed, or transmitted in any form or by any means, including photocopying, recording, or other electronic or mechanical methods.

This publication is sold with the idea that the publisher is not required to render accounting, officially permitted, or otherwise, qualified services. If advice is required, it is necessary to seek the services of a legal or professional, a practiced individual in the profession. This document is geared towards providing substantial and reliable information in regards to the topics covered.

DISCLAIMER

The information written in this book is for educational and entertainment purposes only. Strenuous efforts have been made to provide accurate, up to date and reliable complete information. The information in this book is true and complete to the best of our knowledge. All recommendations are made without guarantee on the part of the author and publisher.

Neither the publisher nor the author takes any responsibility for any possible consequences of reading or enjoying the recipes in this book. The author and publisher disclaim any liability in connection with the use of information contained in this book. Under no circumstance will any legal responsibility or blame be apportioned against the author or publisher for any reparation, damages, or monetary loss due to the information herein, either directly or indirectly.

Table of Contents

CHAPTER 1: INSTANT POT 101 12

INTRODUCTION 12

What is an Instant Pot? 13

Benefits of Using an Instant Pot 14

Making Sense of Those Buttons 15

Instant Pot Must-Have Tools (Accessories) 18

How to Clean Your Instant Pot (Cleaning Tips) 20

Instant Pot FAQ – Frequently Asked Questions 22

    Before Purchasing Instant Pot 22

    After Purchasing Instant Pot 23

Troubleshooting Tips 24

CHAPTER 2: BREAKFAST 26

    Banana Oatmeal 26

    Breakfast Egg Muffins 27

    Sweet Potato Morning Hash 28

    Jamaican Cornmeal Porridge 29

    Vanilla Apple Cinnamon Breakfast Quinoa 30

    Easy Apple Butter 31

    Buckwheat Porridge 32

    Quinoa Blueberry Breakfast Bowl 33

    Regular Oatmeal 34

    French Toast Casserole 35

    Spanish Chorizo & Potato Hash 36

    Vanilla Latte Steel Cut Oats 37

Broccoli Ham & Pepper Frittata 38

Breakfast Cobbler 39

Breakfast Burrito Casserole 40

Steel Cut Oatmeal 42

Creamy Pumpkin Maple Oats 43

Loaded Breakfast Potatoes 44

Quinoa Breakfast Bowls 46

CHAPTER 2: SOUPS & STEWS 47

Minestrone Soup 47

Vegetable Beef Soup 49

Beef and Porcini Mushroom Stew 50

Pot Borscht (Beet Soup) 51

Ground Beef and Potato Soup 52

Chicken Noodle Soup 53

Italian Sausage Stew 55

Chicken Meatball and Kale Soup 57

Chicken-Sweet Potato Stew 59

Paleo Hamburger Soup 60

Tuscan Chicken Stew 61

French Onion Soup 63

Italian Sausage Stew 64

Taco Soup 66

Chicken-Sweet Potato Stew 67

Unstuffed Cabbage Roll Soup 68

CHAPTER 3: EGGS 69

French "Baked" Eggs 69

Bacon and Egg Risotto 70

Poached Egg in Bell Pepper Cup 71

Eggs En Cocotte 72

Mexican Egg Casserole 73

Egg Bake 75

Western Omelet Quiche 77

Cheesy Egg Bake 78

Ham & Egg Casserole 79

Mini Frittatas 80

Spanish Tortilla Potato Egg Frittata, Quiche 81

Hard-Boiled Eggs 83

Crustless Veggie Quiche 84

CHAPTER 4: POULTRY 85

Thai Chicken Rice Bowl 85

Chicken Taco Bowls 87

Orange Chicken 88

Creamy Chicken Noodle Soup 89

Salsa Shredded Chicken 90

Chili-Lime Chicken 91

Cream Cheese Chicken Pasta 92

Buffalo Chicken Lettuce Wraps 93

Chicken Faux Pho 94

Chipotle Chicken Black Beans and Rice 96

Chicken Breasts 97

Indian Butter Chicken 98

BBQ Chicken with Potatoes 99

Shredded Mexican Chicken 100

Pulled Tandoori Chicken 101

Sweet & Sour Chicken Wing 103

Cashew Butter Chicken 104

Salsa Lime Chicken Tacos 105

Buffalo Chicken Lettuce Wraps 106

Lemon Garlic Chicken 107

Faux-Tesserae Chicken 108

Honey Curry Chicken 110

Italian Chicken 111

Chicken Soup 112

Braised Chicken Drumsticks in Tomatillo Sauce 113

Salsa Lime Chicken Tacos 114

CHAPTER 5: FISH & SEAFOODS 115

Creamy Fish Chowder 115

Shrimp and Lentil Stew 116

Coconut Red Curry Shrimp 117

Fish Stew 119

Instant Pot Salmon 121

Fish with Orange & Ginger Sauce 122

Fish Coconut Curry 123

Mediterranean Style Fish 125

Instant Pot Shrimp 126

Lemon Pepper Salmon 127
Drunken Clams 128
Instant Pot Mussels 129
Poached Salmon 130
Pasta with Tuna and Capers 131
New England Fish Chowder 132
Salmon and Veggies 133
Salmon Biryani 134
Shrimp Paella 135
Spicy Pineapple Shrimp 137
Savory Shrimp with Tomatoes and Feta 138
Creamy Chipotle Shrimp Soup 139
Shrimp Risotto 141
Oyster Stew 142

CHAPTER 6: BEEF 143
Homemade Hamburger 143
Cheesesteak Sloppy 144
Beef and Macaroni 145
Instant Pot Spaghetti 147
Meatball Subs 148
Stuffed Pepper Casserole 149
Barbacoa Beef 150
Beef and Potato Au Gratin 151
Beefy Broccoli Rice 152
Vegetable Beef Soup 153

Sweet Potato Chili 154

Instant Pot Goulash 155

Beef Stroganoff 156

Instant Pot Bolognese 157

Instant Pot Picadillo 158

Mongolian Beef 159

Cheeseburger Macaroni 160

CHAPTER 7: PORK 161

Ground Pork Casserole 161

Pork Chops with Gravy 162

Pulled Pork 164

Pork Lettuce Wraps 165

Pork Carnitas 166

Sloppy Joes 167

Pork Chili 168

Pork Green Chili 170

Spicy Pork & Spinach Stew 171

Pork Stew with Fall Vegetables 172

Pork and Hominy Stew 173

Coca-Cola Pulled Pork 174

CHAPTER 8: BEANS, RICE & GRAINS 176

Tomatillo Poblano White Beans 176

Red Beans and Rice 177

Chicken and Brown Rice 178

Rice Pudding 179

Perfect Rice 180

Chickpea Curry with Brown Rice 181

Black Bean & Lentil Chili 183

Steamed Brown Rice 184

Santa Fe Beans and Rice 185

CHAPTER 9: VEGAN & VEGETARIAN 187

Spiced Potato Spinach Lentils 187

Quinoa with Miso, Mushrooms & Peppers 189

Beet Risotto with Thyme & Goat's Cheese 191

Carrot Lemongrass & Cilantro Soup 193

Barbacoa Mushroom Tacos 194

Vegan Lasagna Soup 196

Chickpea Spinach Curry 198

Sweet Potato Lentil Curry 200

Vegan Mashed Potatoes 202

Jackfruit Curry 204

Pad Thai 206

CHAPTER: 10 SIDE DISHES 208

Rhubarb-Strawberry Compote with Fresh Mint 208

Mac & Cheese 209

Swedish Meatball 210

Thai Chicken Rice Bowl 212

Instant Pot Lasagna 213

Spicy Creamed Corn 215

Gobi Masala 216

Creamy Garlic Broccoli Mash 217

Cilantro Lime Cauliflower Rice 218

Potato Salad 219

Salmon with Chili-Lime Sauce 220

Summer Picnic Potato Salad 221

CHAPTER 11: APPETIZERS 223

Jalapeno Hot Popper & Chicken Dip 223

Prosciutto-Wrapped Asparagus Canes 224

White Queso Dip 225

Easy Artichokes 226

Dr. Pepper Barbecue Meatballs 227

Hawaiian Meatballs 228

Buffalo Chicken Dip 229

Sweet BBQ Meatballs 230

CHAPTER 12: DESSERTS 231

Lemon Cream Pie 231

Apple Cider 232

Applesauce 233

Mini-Lemon Cheesecakes 234

Pineapple Upside-Down Cake 236

Caramel Flan 237

Rhubarb-Strawberry Compote with Fresh Mint 238

Carrot Nut Bread 239

Cocoa Apple Bundt Cake 240

NY Cherry Cheesecake with Ricotta 241

Instant Pot Salsa 242

Sweet and Spicy Meatballs 243

Hawaiian Meatballs 244

White Queso Dip 245

Cheddar Bacon Ale Dip 246

Buffalo Chicken Dip 247

Crispy Chicken Wings 249

Stuffed Peppers 250

Potato Corn Chowder 252

Apple Pie Steel Cut Oats 253

Creamy Macaroni and Cheese 254

Acknowledgement 255

CHAPTER 1: INSTANT POT 101

INTRODUCTION

My passion for pressure cooking runs deep. If you have cooked with a pressure cooker, then you will be familiar with this kitchen appliance. It is a multi-cooker that performs more than functions. The Instant Pot enables you to cook a wide variety of dishes including meat, fish, eggs, grain, poultry, beans, cakes, yogurt and vegetables etc. What makes the Instant Pot exceptional is because you can use different cooking programs such as a steamer, rice cooker, sauté pan, and even a warming pot, thus saving more time, money, and space than buying any other kitchen appliances.

The Instant Pot serves as a multi-use programmable appliance can help create easy, fast and flavorful recipes with the ability to apply different cooking settings all in one pot. It was developed by clever Canadian technology experts seeking to be the ultimate kitchen mate, from stir-frying, pressure cooking, slow cooking and yogurt and cake making. It was created to serve as a one-stop shop to allow home cooks prepare a tasty meal with the press of a button. You can cook almost everything in your Instant Pot.

In this book, we will explore the variety of easy delicious dishes you can cook with your Instant Pot. We will explore a wide variety of dishes, from breakfast to dinner, soups to stews, desserts to appetizers, meat to beef, side dishes to vegetables and use a healthy ingredient in the process. The vast majority of the recipes can be prepared and served in less than 45 minutes. Each recipe is written with the exact preparation time, cooking instructions and ingredients required to prepare the dishes. Once you try these delicious dishes with our cookbook, you and your Instant Pot are sure to become inseparable too.

What is an Instant Pot?

The Instant Pot is a multifunctional cooker that acts as a slow cooker, rice cooker, steamer, electric pressure cooker, sauté pan and a yogurt maker. It is a single device or multi-cooker that does the job of seven different kitchen appliances ranging from electric pressure cooker, rice cooker, steamer, yogurt maker, sauté pan, and warming pot etc. It makes use of a combination of steam and pressure which enables your foods to cook quicker and safer than other devices. It is a programmable countertop multi-cooker which speeds up cooking by 2~6 times using up to 70% less energy.

The Instant Pot can cook nutritious healthy food in a convenient and consistent fashion, making everything from slow-and-low barbecue dishes and tenders stews to perfectly prepared rice pilaf, lentil, bacon, chicken and steamed veggies. You can rely on Instant Pot more than any other kitchen appliances and it deserves to earn a spot in your kitchen.

The Instant Pot is a versatile multi-cooker that can do the job of a pressure cooker, slow cooker, rice cooker, steamer, poultry and more. It has lots of safety features which makes it safer to use and comes in different models. It comes with preset programs that are specifically designed to cook your food to perfection, whether it be a cheesecake, a stew, soup, or porridge.

Benefits of Using an Instant Pot

1 Saving Time & Energy:

The Instant Pot cook foods much faster than any other traditional methods of cooking. Electric pressure cooker can reduce cooking time by up to 70% when compared with other methods. Cooking with an Instant Pot requires less water used in cooking and a fully insulated external pot, much less energy is required thereby saving up to 70% of energy comparing with boiling, steaming, and slow cooking.

You will save more time and money when cooking with an Instant Pot. A whole chicken can be cooked in just half an hour, make a tender pot roast in less than 2 hours, cook a large squash in just 10 minutes and veggies in less than 5 thereby saving more time and energy.

2 Preserving Nutrients & Cook Tasty Food:

Pressure cooking ensures that heat is evenly and quickly distributed. The food is not necessarily required to be immersed in water, it simply requires sufficient water to keep the pressure cooker filled with steam. This will not allow the vitamins and minerals to be leached or dissolved away by water. Since the food is surrounded by the steam, the foods will not be oxidized by air exposure at heat, so asparagus, lentil, broccoli, artichoke, and other veggies retain their bright green colors and phytochemical. It will also enable the food to retains its original flavor.

Scientific studies have proved that pressure cooking is the best method for retaining the vitamins and minerals of the food that your body needs. Pressure cooking broccoli, for instance, will retain 90% of its vitamin C. The retention when compared to boiling is (66% retention) or steaming (78%). Instant Pot tends to be the healthier option.

3 Eliminating Harmful Micro-Organisms in Food:

Pressure cookers cook foods at a temperature above the boiling point of water, killing almost all harmful living micro-organisms such as bacteria, fungi, and viruses. It helps to kill harmful micro-organisms that are toxic to our health. Some foods such as rice, wheat, corn and beans may carry fungal poisons called aflatoxins.

Aflatoxins are naturally occurring mycotoxins produced by many species of Aspergillus fungi, as a result of improper storage, such as in humid conditions. Research has proved that aflatoxins are a potent trigger of liver cancer and may play a vital role in a host of other cancers too. Aflatoxins cannot be destroyed by just heating your food to the boiling point, they can only be destroyed by pressure cooking.

4 Helps Boost Digestibility of Foods:

I believe you must have heard, "You are what you eat." But actually, you are what you absorb from your food. Boosting the digestibility of your food will maximize the nutritional value to your body. Pressure cooking makes even the toughest meats moist and tender, which is the key to foods that your body can easily digest.

Making Sense of Those Buttons

1. **Soup:**

The Instant Pot has a soup program that is 30 minutes on High Pressure. But this program depends on if you are using fresh or frozen meats. The soup times may range from 20 minutes to an hour. The soup function cooks at High Pressure for about 30 minutes. It can be Adjusted to more to cook for about 40 minutes. It can also be Adjusted to less to cook for about 20 minutes.

2. **Meat / Stew:**

The meat / stew program is 20 minutes on High Pressure. Though, the times may vary wildly depending on temperature, size, and thickness of the meats. The Meat / Stew function cooks at High Pressure for about 35 minutes. It can be Adjusted to more cooks for 45 minutes and Adjusted to less cooks for about 20 minutes.

3. **Bean / Chili:**

The Bean / Chili program is 30 minutes on High Pressure. The Bean / Chili button cooks at High Pressure for 30 minutes. It can be Adjusted to more cooks for about 40 minutes. The button can also be Adjusted to less cooks for about 25 minutes.

4. **Poultry:**

The poultry button is 12 minutes on High Pressure. This cooking time is meant for uncooked chicken in small portions. Larger chicken pieces will need a cooking time of about 25 minutes to reach a center temperature of 165°F. The Poultry function cooks at High Pressure for 15 minutes. The button can be Adjusted to more cooks for about 30 minutes and Adjusted to less cooks for about 5 minutes.

5. **Slow Cook:**

The Slow Cook button can be programmed from between 30 minutes to 20 hours. The pressure cooking time can be lowered up to 24 hours. The Slow Cook mode can be set to normal (which is equivalent to low), more (which is equivalent to high), or less (which is equivalent to keep warm mode).

6. **Sauté:**

The sauté button can be used to brown your meat directly inside of your Instant Pot. The temperature of the sauté button can be adjusted by using the 'Adjust' function to cycle through the modes of less, normal, and more. The temperature mode has to be adjusted within 10 seconds of pressing the sauté mode. When you press the Sauté function, kindly wait until it displays "Hot" before adding ingredients to the pot.

7. **Pressure:**

The pressure button serves as a toggle between low and High-Pressure modes. It can simply be used to switch between High and low-pressure settings for pressure cooking programs.

8 Manual:

The Manual button can be used to start pressure cooking. It can be switched between low and high pressure by using the 'pressure' button within 10 seconds of pressing the 'Manual' button. You can set a pressure level and cook time using the Adjust and [+] or [-] buttons. When the time is up, time will begin to count down.

9 Adjust:

This button can be used to adjust the temperature of the slow cooking and sauté settings between less, normal, and more. This button can be used to toggle from the Less, Normal and More settings on older Instant Pot versions. You can select any of the feature you wish to use and press Adjust until the light under Less, Normal and More is adjusted to the desired setting.

10 Timer:

The timer setting is for programmed delayed cooking. The button performs the function for both slow cooking mode and regular pressure cooking mode. This setting must be pressed within 10 seconds of setting your cooking program's time and can be adjusted by pressing the + and – buttons.

11 Keep warm / Cancel:

The Keep Warm button sets the unit into keep warm mode, and another less turns the unit OFF. This setting helps to turn the Auto Keep Warm function ON and OFF. The Keep Warm function keeps the foods in your cooking pot between 145–172°F. This button can also be used to cancel a function or to turn off the Instant Pot.

12 Yogurt:

This function is not included in the IP-LUX series and is a fully-automated program. These settings can be sued to make yogurt. You can press this button and Adjust to More for boiling the milk and use Normal for incubating the yogurt.

13 Steam:

This button cooks at High Pressure for about 10 minutes. It can be Adjusted to more cooks for about 15 minutes and Adjusted to less for about 3 minutes. The Steam function is simply normal High-Pressure mode that can be set all the way down to 0 minutes. It simply means that once the cooking time is up, you can perform a quick release. This function is very important when cooking leafy vegetables and preventing them from being overcooked.

14 Porridge and Multigrain:

The Porridge button cooks at High Pressure for 20 minutes. It can be Adjusted to more cooks for 30 minutes and Adjusted to less cooks for 15 minutes.

15 Multigrain:

The Multigrain button cooks at High Pressure for 40 minutes. It can be Adjusted to more cooks for 45 minutes and pressure cooking time of 60 minutes. It can also be Adjusted to less cooks for 20 minutes.

16 Rice:

The Rice button is an automated program that begins at 12 minutes. This button functions at low pressure and can cook white or jasmine rice in 20 minutes flat. The setting is specifically designed for cooking white rice and the cooking time can be adjusted depending on the quantity of water and rice in the cooking pot.

17 Egg:

The Egg button cooks at High Pressure for 5 minutes. The button can be Adjusted to more cooks for 6 minutes and Adjusted to less cooks for about 4 minutes.

18 Cake:

The Cake button cooks at High Pressure for 30 minutes. It can be Adjusted to more cooks for 40 minutes and Adjusted to less cooks for about 25 minutes.

Instant Pot Must-Have Tools (Accessories)

The Instant Pot comes along with lots of accessories. You might need to buy more accessories to get the most out of your meals:

1. **Silicone Egg Mold:**

The silicon egg mold will work in your 5,6,8-quart pressure cookers. It can be used for storing smaller portions and includes a sealing lid.

2. **Silicone Mini Mitts:**

It is advisable to protect your fingers with the mini mitts. The cooking pot usually gets hot when cooking, the mini mitts set can be used to protect your hands when lifting items out of your pressure cooker.

3. **Silicone Vegetable Steamer and Lifter:**

The steamer / lifter keeps your veggies off the heated bottom of your pressure cooker. The steamer handles can be used to lift items easily from the pressure cooker. It also works great in your microwave. It can be used to lift a whole chicken out of your Instant Pot without it falling apart.

4. **7-inch Spring Form Non-Stick Pan:**

The spring form pan can be used for baking. It is great for baking cakes, cheesecakes, and bread. These sizes will fit into your pressure cooker 5,6,8 quarts.

5. **Cook's Stainless-Steel Steamer Basket / Colander:**

Most pressure cookers don't come with this basket! These tool helps to keep your food items off the bottom heating element and out of the water. Food items such as pasta do not require draining when cooking in a pressure cooker but having the pasta in this basket helps to easily lift the pasta from the pressure cooker.

6. **Clear lid:**

The clear lid comes with a steam vent and handle. It is used for sautéing or slow-cooking. It comes in 3, 6, and 8-quart sizes.

7. **Extra Silicone Rings:**

The extra silicone rings are needed on hand at all times. It can be used to switch out rings depending on whether you're cooking a sweet or savory dish. They usually wear out after multiple uses, but it's helpful an extra just in case.

8. **Steaming Rack:**

The steaming rack can be used to steam your veggies, pot-stickers, proteins, anything!

9. **Mesh steaming basket:**

This is another helpful variation of a steamer. The mesh steaming basket can be used for steaming, frying, straining. It can be used for many things and functions out of just one product.

10. **Extra Stainless Steel:**

It makes it easier to prepare multiple dishes. You just have to switch out the pots rather than cleaning one over and over again.

11. **Cheesecake pan:**

The cheesecake pan can be used for making cheesecake in your Instant Pot. Yep, it's true. Plus, the bottom is removable but doesn't leak can be used for dessert after steaming all the veggies.

12. **Instant Read Digital Meat Thermometer:**

This thermometer can used for measuring the heat content in meat. Having the Meat Thermometer on hand puts an end to serving undercooked or over cooked protein. It can also be used for daily cooking or grilling.

How to Clean Your Instant Pot (Cleaning Tips)

It is important to clean your Instant Pot right after dinner or right after you're done using it, because:

- The spills, drips, etc. are still warm and clean up more easily when cleaning right away.
- You'll appreciate it being clean the next time you're ready to use it.

What NOT to do when cleaning your Instant Pot:

Ensure that you clean your Instant Pot right after cook and avoid the following practices when cleaning:

- Do not submerge the base in water.
- Do not leave it plugged in while cleaning it.

Tools you will need when cleaning your Instant Pot include:

- Washcloth
- Non-scratch scouring pad
- Towel
- Dish soap or all-purpose spray cleaner
- Vinegar
- Baking soda
- Toothbrush or small cleaning brushes

How to Clean Your Instant Pot:

1. Fill a sink with hot, soapy water. This step is the most important because it will make everything easier and faster.

2. Ensure that you unplug your Instant Pot and remove the insert pot from the base.

3. The next step is to place everything that needs to be cleaned in the hot, soapy water. Dump out any liquid that must have accumulated in the condensation cup. Place the silicone ring, valve cover if your model has a removable valve cover, sealing valve, and lid in the soapy water.

4. Dip a small cleaning utensil such as toothbrush or small cleaning brush in the hot, soapy water. Use the brush to clean all the nooks and crannies of the base. Make use of a wet, wrung-out cloth in sopping up any liquids or dislodged food particles. The toothbrush and the washcloth can be uses to reach and dislodge everything.

5. Use a washcloth and all-purpose spray cleaner to wipe down the outside of the Instant Pot to look pretty and shiny.

6. Wash everything that's been soaking in the hot, soapy water. After washing, rinse and air dry with the towel.

7. Scrub the silicone ring with the toothbrush. Use baking soda to remove any odor and staining. You can soak the silicon ring in vinegar water for a few hours if it's still stinky. Rinse and air dry after washing.

8. Scrub the inside of the insert pot in circular motion with non-scratch scouring pad. Make use of baking soda for stubborn messes.

9. Scrub the following accessories with toothbrush — the lid, sealing valve, condensation cup and wipe with a towel.

Instant Pot FAQ – Frequently Asked Questions

Before Purchasing Instant Pot:

The answers to Frequently Asked Questions before purchasing an Instant Pot are listed below:

1. What is an Instant Pot? Is it the same as a pressure cooker?

Yes, the Instant Pot is the same as the pressure cooker and is currently one of the most popular electric pressure cooker brands. It is a multi-functional cooker and has some extra functions such as rice cooker, soup, poultry, meat, yogurt, sauté pan etc.

2. Does the Instant Pot really speed up the cooking process?

Pressure cooking is always faster and saves time. The fast cooking process may not be noticeable for some foods like broccoli or shrimps. Foods such as pulled pork can be done in under 90 minutes, when it usually takes about 2 to 4 hours to make in the oven.

3. Are there any disadvantages with cooking in the Instant Pot?

The disadvantage involved in cooking with any pressure cooker is you can't inspect, taste, or adjust the food along the way. That's why it's necessary to follow the exact recipes instructions with accurate cooking times.

4. Is Instant Pot safe to use?

Most modern electric pressure cookers like the Instant Pot are quiet, very safe and easy to use. The Instant Pot has about 10 UL Certified proven safety mechanisms to avoid some of the potential issues. It has lots of safety features to prevent potential issues.

5. What is Instant Pot's working pressure?

The Instant Pot working pressure is within the range of 10.15~11.6 psi.

6. Can Instant Pot be used for Pressure Canning?

No, the Instant Pot has not been tested for food safety in pressure canning. The cooking programs in Instant Pot IP-CSG, IP-LUX and IP-DUO series are regulated by a pressure sensor instead of a thermometer, the elevation of your location can disrupt the actual cooking temperature. For that very reason, it is not advisable to use your Instant Pot for pressure canning purpose.

7. Can I use the Instant Pot for Pressure Frying?

We would not recommend pressure frying in any electric pressure cookers. The pressure cooker gasket may be melted by the splattering oil.

After Purchasing Instant Pot:

1. What kind of Instant Pot accessories do you recommend?

There is hand-picked list of accessories we would recommend. The accessories include steamer baskets, meat thermometers, silicon egg mold, cheesecake pan, steaming rack etc.

2. What kind of accessories or containers can I use in the Instant Pot?

Any oven-safe accessories and containers can be used in your Instant Pot. Always have in mind that different materials will conduct heat differently and this will make the cooking times to vary. Always use stainless steel containers as they quickly conduct heat.

3. I just got my Instant Pot. What should I do first?

Congratulations and welcome to the party! Conduct an initial test run before cooking with your Instant Pot.

4. How to do a Quick Release?

When the cooking cycle is up, carefully move the venting knob from sealing position to venting position. It usually takes a few minutes and rapidly releases the pressure in the pressure cooker. Exercise some patient and wait until the floating valve completely drops before opening the lid.

5. How to do a Natural Release?

When the cooking cycle is up, you have to wait until the floating valve completely drops before opening the lid. Carefully turn the venting knob from sealing position to venting position. It will enable all the pressure to release before opening the lid. Natural pressure release usually takes about 10 – 25 minutes.

Troubleshooting Tips

Here is a list of instructions to carry out when troubleshooting:

1. **Rice is half cooked or too hard:**

Possible Reason: The rice contained too little water

Solution: Ensure that the dry rice and water ratio is adjusted according to recipe instructions.

Possible Reason: The Instant Pot lid is removed too early

Solution: When the cooking cycle is up, leave the lid on for additional 5 minutes.

2. **Rice is too soft:**

Possible Reason: The rice contained too much water.

Solution: Ensure that the dry rice and water ratio is adjusted according to recipe instructions.

3. **Difficulty with closing lid:**

Possible Reason: The sealing ring is not properly closed.

Solution: Carefully position the sealing ring to stay tightly in place.

Possible Reason: The float valve may be in popped-up position.

Solution: Gently press down the float to stay in place.

4. **Difficulty with opening lid:**

Possible Reason: Pressure inside the cooker

Solution: When the cooking cycle is complete, position the steam release handle to the venting position to release the internal pressure. Carefully remove the lid after the pressure is completely released.

Possible Reason: The float valve stuck at the popped-up position thereby causing difficulties in opening the lid.

Solution: Carefully press the float valve with a pen or long utensil to open the lid.

5. **Float valve unable to rise:**

Possible Reason: This may result when there is too little food or water in inner pot.

Solution: Pour water according to the recipe instructions.

Possible Reason: The float valve may be blocked by the lid locking pin.

Solution: Completed close the lid completely to prevent the steam from coming out from the steam valve.

Possible Reason: The Steam release valve may not be placed in sealing position.

Solution: Move the steam release handle to the sealing position.

6. **Steam leaks from the side of the lid:**

Possible Reason: There is no sealing ring in place.

Solution: Carefully install the sealing ring in place.

Possible Reason: The sealing ring might also be damaged.

Solution: Replace the damaged sealing ring with a new one.

Possible Reason: There might be some particles of food debris attached to the sealing ring.

Solution: Clean the sealing ring to remove any attached food debris.

7. **Steam leaks from float valve for over 2 minutes:**

Possible Reason: Some particles of food debris may be attached on the float valve silicone seal.

Solution: Clean the float valve silicone seal to remove any attached food debris.

Possible Reason: The float valve silicone ring may be worn- out.

Solution: Replace the worn-out float valve silicone ring with a new one.

CHAPTER 2: BREAKFAST

Banana Oatmeal

Preparation time: 5 minutes

Cooking time: 20 minutes

Total time: 25 minutes

Serves: 2

Ingredients:

- 1 cup of water
- 1 cup of milk (we used 1% fat milk)
- ½ cup of steel cut oats
- ¼ tsp. of cinnamon powder
- ½ of a large banana, mashed
- 1 to 2 tbsp of brown sugar, adjust to taste
- Splash of vanilla extract

Cooking Instructions:

1. Spray the inner liner of your Instant Pot with a non-stick spray.

2. Add the water, milk, steel cut oats, cinnamon powder. Place the mashed banana on top and don't stir.

3. Close and lock the lid in place and ensure that the valve is in sealing position. Select the "Porridge" function and set the time to 15 minutes.

4. When the timer beeps, use a quick pressure release. Carefully remove the lid and give everything a good stir.

5. Add the brown sugar (or your desired sweetener). Give everything a good mix until combined. Add a splash of vanilla extract and mix again.

6. Place the banana oatmeal into individual platter and top with sliced bananas, peanut butter, sliced almonds or your desired topping.

7. Serve and enjoy!

Breakfast Egg Muffins

Preparation time: 15 minutes

Cook time: 12 minutes

Total time: 27 minutes

Servings: 6

Ingredients:

- 8 large eggs
- ¼ cup (60 ml milk), we used unsweetened almond milk
- ¼ tsp. of salt
- 1/8 tsp. of fresh ground black pepper
- 1 cup (30 g) of fresh baby spinach, chopped
- ½ cup (90 g) of diced seeded tomato
- 2 scallions white and green parts, sliced
- 1/3 cup (26.6g) shredded Parmesan cheese

Cooking Instructions:

1. Generously spray a 6-ounce ovenproof custard cups with a nonstick cooking spray.
2. In a medium bowl, whisk together the eggs, milk, salt, and pepper until blended.
3. Carefully divide the spinach, tomato, and scallions among the 6 custard cups.
4. Pour the egg mixture over the veggies and sprinkle the Parmesan over each cup.
5. Pour 1 cup (235 ml) of water into the Instant Pot and place a trivet in the bottom.
6. Place 3 custard cups on the trivet and gently place the second trivet on top. Carefully place the remaining 3 cups on it.
7. Close and lock the lid in place. Select High Pressure and set to cook for about 6 minutes.
8. When the time is up, turn off the Instant Pot. Allow the pressure to release naturally for about 5 minutes.
9. Open the lid when the valve drops and carefully remove the cups.
10. Serve and enjoy.

Sweet Potato Morning Hash

Preparation time: 10 mins

Cooking time: 10 mins

Total time: 20 mins

Servings: 4

Ingredients:

- 6 large eggs
- 1 tbsp. of Italian seasoning
- 1/2 tsp. of sea salt
- 1/2 tsp. of ground black pepper
- 1/2 lb. of ground pork sausage
- 1 large sweet potato, peeled and cubed
- 1 small onion, peeled and diced
- 2 cloves of garlic, minced
- 1 medium green bell pepper, seeded and diced
- 2 cups of water

Cooking Instructions:

1. Whisk eggs, Italian seasoning, pepper and salt together in a medium bowl and set aside

2. Press the Sauté button on your Instant Pot. Stir-fry sausage, sweet potato, onion, garlic, and bell pepper together for 3 to 5 minutes until onions are translucent.

3. Add the mixture to a 7-cup greased glass dish and pour the whisked eggs over the sausage mixture.

4. Place steamer rack in your Instant Pot and pour in water. Place dish with egg mixture onto steamer rack.

5. Close the lid and ensure that the valve is in sealing position. Select Manual function to cook on High-Pressure for about 5 minutes.

6. When timer beeps, do a quick pressure release until float valve drops. then open the lid carefully.

7. Remove dish from Instant Pot. Let sit at room temperature for 4 to 10 minutes to allow the eggs to set properly.

8. Serve and enjoy!

Jamaican Cornmeal Porridge

Preparation time: 5 minutes

Cooking Time: 20 minutes

Total Time: 25 minutes

Serves: 4

Ingredients:

- 4 cups of water, separated
- 1 cup of milk
- 1 cup of yellow cornmeal, fine
- 2 sticks cinnamon
- 3 pimento berries
- 1 teaspoon of vanilla extract
- ½ teaspoon of nutmeg, ground
- ½ cup of sweetened condensed milk

Cooking Instructions:

1. First, set your Instant Pot on porridge setting for 6 minutes.

2. Add the 3 cups of water and 1 cup of milk to your Instant Pot.

3. Whisk 1 cup of water and cornmeal properly in a separate bowl, Add to your instant pot and whisk.

4. Add the cinnamon sticks, pimento berries, nutmeg and vanilla extract. Cover the Lid and allow to cook for 6 minutes.

5. When time is up, use a natural pressure release and allow to release pressure.

6. Once done with natural pressure release, then add sweetened condensed milk to sweeten.

7. Serve and enjoy!

Vanilla Apple Cinnamon Breakfast Quinoa

Preparation time: 5 minutes

Cooking time: 1 minutes

Total time: 6 minutes

Serves: 4

Ingredients:

- 1 cup of quinoa
- 1 ½ cup of water
- ¼ teaspoon of mineral salt
- 1 chopped apple
- 2 tablespoons of cinnamon
- ½ teaspoon of vanilla
- ¼ cup gentle sweet

Cooking Instructions:

1. Add all ingredients to your Instant Pot and stir thoroughly.

2. Secure the lid in place and ensure that the valve is in sealing position.

3. Select Manual function to cook on High-Pressure for about 1 minute.

4. When time is up, do a natural pressure release for about 8 minutes.

5. Carefully open the lid and stir.

6. Serve and enjoy!

Easy Apple Butter

Preparation time: 15 minutes

Cooking time: 1 hour

Total time: 1 hour 15 minutes

Ingredients:

- 5 pounds of apples
- ½ cup of brown sugar
- ¼ teaspoon of ground cloves
- ½ teaspoon of ground nutmeg
- 1 tablespoon of cinnamon
- pinch of salt
- 2 tablespoons of apple cider vinegar
- 1 tablespoon of vanilla extract
- ¼ cup water

Cooking Instructions:

1. Add all the ingredients in your pressure cooker and mix them properly.
2. Close and lock the lid in place.
3. Select Manual function to cook on High-Pressure for about 1 hour.
4. Allow the pressure cooker to release pressure naturally and carefully remove the lid.
5. Use the immersion blender to blend the apple smoothly, then pour into the jar.
6. Keep the apple butter for about 3 weeks in the refrigerator.
7. Serve and enjoy!

Buckwheat Porridge

Preparation time: 5 minutes

Cook time: 25 minutes

Total time: 30 minutes

Serves: 4 to 5

Ingredients:

- 1 cup of raw buckwheat groats
- 3 cups of rice milk
- 1 banana, sliced
- ¼ cup raisins
- 1 teaspoon of ground cinnamon
- ½ teaspoon vanilla
- Chopped nuts, optional

Cooking Instructions:

1. Rinse buckwheat and add in your Instant Pot.

2. Add the rice milk, banana, raisins, vanilla and cinnamon. Close and lock the lid in place.

3. Ensure that the steam release is in the closed position.

4. Select Manual function to cook on High-Pressure for about 6 minutes.

5. When time is up, turn off the pot and allow time for the natural pressure release for about 20 minutes.

6. After pressure is released, carefully open the Lid of your Instant Pot and stir porridge with a long-handled spoon.

7. Add more rice milk to individual servings to achieve preferred consistency.

8. Sprinkle with chopped nuts if desired.

9. Serve and enjoy!

Quinoa Blueberry Breakfast Bowl

Preparation time: 5 minutes

Cook time: 1 minute

Total time: 6 minutes

Serves: 4

Ingredients:

- 1 ½ cups of white quinoa
- 1 ½ cups of water
- 1 cinnamon stick
- ¼ cup of raisins
- 1 tbsp of honey plus more for serving
- ¾ cup of grated apple
- 1 cup of cold-pressed apple juice
- 1 cup of plain yogurt plus more for serving
- ¼ cup of chopped pistachios
- Blueberries to serve

Cooking Instructions:

1. Use a fine mesh strainer to rinse the quinoa. Put the quinoa, cinnamon stick and water to your Instant Pot.

2. Close and lock the Lid in place, make sure the vent is set to sealing. Select Manual function to cook on High-Pressure for about 1 minute.

3. When time is up, allow the pressure release naturally for about 10 minutes and then do a quick pressure release.

4. Transfer the quinoa into a medium size bowl, then remove the cinnamon stick and allow to cool.

5. Put the, honey, raisins, apple and apple juice and stir to combine properly. Then refrigerate for 1 hour.

6. Add the yogurt and stir to combine. Serve topped with yogurt, pistachios, blueberries and honey.

7. Serve and enjoy!

Regular Oatmeal

Preparation time: 5 minutes

Cook time: 5 minutes

Total time: 10 minutes

Serves: 4

Ingredients:

- 1 cup of oats (use steel oats if you like)
- 2 ½ cup of water
- 1 cup of apple skinned and diced
- 2 tablespoons of brown sugar
- 3 tablespoons of butter
- Pinch of cinnamon
- Raisins, optional

Cooking Instructions:

1. Set your Instant Pot on Manual High Pressure.

2. Add the butter and allow to melt. Then, turn off your instant pot.

3. Add the water, oats, brown sugar, apples, cinnamon and raisins if desired.

4. Stir the ingredients properly. Close the Lid and the steam valve, set to manual high pressure for 5 minutes.

5. When time is up, do a quick release.

6. Serve and enjoy!

French Toast Casserole

Ingredients:

- 3 eggs
- 1 cup of half and half cream
- ½ cup of milk
- 1 tbsp. of cinnamon
- 1 tsp. of vanilla
- 1 loaf of French bread cubed
- ½ cup of blueberries

Cooking Instructions:

1. Generously spray the inside of your pot with nonstick cooking spray.
2. Cube the bread and place in the Instant Pot.
3. In a medium bowl, whisk together the milk, cream, cinnamon, vanilla and eggs.
4. Pour the custard mixture over the bread cubes and turn to coat evenly.
5. Sprinkle in the blueberries. Close and lock the lid in place.
6. Cook for about 15 minutes on Manual High Pressure.
7. When the time is up, use a natural pressure release for about 10 minutes.
8. Serve and enjoy!

Spanish Chorizo & Potato Hash

Preparation time: 5 minutes

Cook time: 15 minutes

Total time: 20 minutes

Servings: 4

Ingredients:

- 6 large potatoes
- 1 chorizo sausage
- 4 slices back bacon
- 1 onion, peeled and diced
- 250 g of soft cheese
- 2 tablespoons of Greek yoghurt
- 1 tablespoon of garlic puree
- 1 tablespoon of olive oil
- 200 ml of vegetable stock
- 3 tablespoons of rosemary
- 3 tablespoons of basil
- Salt & pepper to taste

Cooking Instructions:

1. Place the onion, garlic and olive oil into the bottom of your Instant Pot.

2. Press the sauté setting and sauté the onions until it has softened.

3. Peel and dice the potatoes and slice the sausages and add in the Instant Pot.

4. Give everything a good a stir and add a little drop of olive oil.

5. Slice the bacon into chunks, add the seasoning and cook for a few minutes.

6. Add the stock and select the soup setting to cook for about 10 minutes.

7. Set the valve to sealing position. When the time is up, use a natural pressure release for about 10 minutes. Drain the stock water and remove the potatoes.

8. In a medium bowl, add some herbs and mix in the soft cheese and Greek yoghurt.

9. Serve and enjoy!

Vanilla Latte Steel Cut Oats

Servings: 4

Ingredients:

- 2 ½ cups of water
- 1 cup of milk
- 1 cup of steel cut oats
- 2 tbsp. of sugar
- 1 tsp. of espresso powder
- ¼ tsp. of salt
- 2 tsp. of vanilla extract
- Freshly whipped cream
- Finely grated chocolate

Cooking Instructions:

1. Add water, milk, oats, sugar, espresso powder, and salt to the bottom of your Instant Pot.

2. Give everything a good stir to dissolve the espresso powder.

3. Close and lock the lid in place. Select High Pressure and set to cook for about 10 minutes.

4. When the time is up, turn off the Instant Pot and use a natural pressure release for about 10 minutes.

5. After 10 minutes, do a quick pressure release to release any remaining pressure.

6. Carefully remove the lid when the valve drops. Stir in vanilla extract and more sugar to taste.

7. Cover and allow it to sit for about 5 minutes until the oats achieves your desired thickness.

8. Serve topped with whipped cream and grated chocolate.

Broccoli Ham & Pepper Frittata

Preparation time: 10 minutes

Cook time: 30 minutes

Total time: 40 minutes

Servings: 4

Ingredients:

- 8 oz. of ham cubed
- 1 cup of sweet peppers sliced
- 2 cups of frozen broccoli
- 4 eggs
- 1 cup of half and half
- 1 cup of shredded cheddar cheese
- 1 teaspoon of salt
- 2 tsp. of ground pepper

Cooking Instructions:

1. Generously grease a 6 x 3 pan with nonstick cooking spray.

2. Arrange the sliced sweet peppers in the bottom of the pan and add the cubed ham on top. Cover with the frozen broccoli.

3. In a medium bowl, whisk together the eggs, half and half, salt, and pepper to taste. Stir in shredded cheese and pour the egg mixture on top of the vegetables and ham.

4. Cover the content with foil. Add 2 cups of water in the inner liner of your Instant Pot.

5. Place a steamer rack on top and carefully place the covered pan on the steamer rack.

6. Cook on High Pressure for about 20 minutes. When the time is up, allow it to release pressure naturally for 10 minutes. Allow it to sit for about 5-10 minutes.

7. Use a knife to loosen the side, place a plate on top of the pan, and thump out the frittata onto the plate.

8. Flip it on a plate and broil for about 3-4 minutes to melt the cheese.

9. Serve and enjoy.

Breakfast Cobbler

Serves: 2

Ingredients:

- 1 pear, diced
- 1 apple, diced
- 1 plum, diced
- 2 tablespoons of local honey
- 3 (45 ml) tablespoons coconut oil
- ½ teaspoon of ground cinnamon
- ¼ cup of unsweetened shredded coconut
- ¼ cup of pecan pieces
- 2 tablespoons of sunflower seeds, we salted and roasted it
- Coconut whipped cream, optional for garnishing

Cooking Instructions:

1. Place the cut fruit into the stainless steel of your Instant Pot.

2. Spoon in the honey and coconut oil and sprinkle the cinnamon.

3. Close and lock the lid in place. Ensure that the valve is set to the sealing position.

4. Select the Steam button and set to cook for about 10 minutes.

5. When the time is up, use a quick pressure release.

6. Carefully open the lid and transfer the cooked fruit with a slotted spoon or skimmer into a serving bowl.

7. Place the coconut, pecans, and sunflower seeds into the residual liquid and click the Sauté button.

8. Let the contents to cook, shifting them regularly to cook evenly.

9. Immediately they are nicely browned and toasted for about 5 minutes, remove them and place them on top of the cooked fruit.

10. Serve warm and topped with coconut whipped cream if desired.

Breakfast Burrito Casserole

Preparation time: 10 minutes

Cook time: 13 minutes

Total time: 23 minutes

Yield: 6 tacos

Ingredients:

- 4 eggs
- 2 lb. of red potatoes, cubed
- ¼ cup of chopped white or yellow onion
- 1 diced jalapeno
- 6 ounces of ham steak cubed
- ½ teaspoon of salt
- ½ teaspoon of mesquite seasoning
- ¼ teaspoon of chili powder
- ¾ teaspoon of taco seasoning

Burrito toppings:

- Salsa, avocado, hot sauce and marinated red onions.
- Tortillas, we used the new Siete coconut flour

Cooking Instructions:

1. Mix together the salt, seasonings, eggs and 1 tablespoon of water in a large bowl.

2. Gently beat the egg until the yokes are broken up.

3. Add the onions, potatoes or cheese, ham and jalapeno to the bowl.

4. Add the mixture to the pot to place inside the Instant Pot. Make use of a lid or a foil to cover the pot.

5. Add 1 cup of water to the bottom of the Instant Pot and place the trivet to the bottom of your Instant Pot.

6. Carefully place the covered pan with the egg mixture on the trivet. Set the pot to the sealing position and cook on Manual for about 13 minutes.

7. When the time is up, use a natural pressure release. Open the lid and remove the pan from your Instant Pot.

8. Fill the burritos and heat up the tortillas in a skillet for some seconds on each side.

9. In each burrito, add a few scoops of the egg mixtures, a slice of avocado, salsa and red onions.

10. Wrap up and enjoy!

Steel Cut Oatmeal

Ingredients:

- 1 cup of steel cut oats
- 2 ½ to 3 of cups water

Optional Toppings:

- Strawberries, bananas, blueberries, apples, pears, chopped dates, cinnamon, flax seed, flax seed, coconut flakes, peanut butter, maple syrup or agave etc.

Cooking Instructions:

1. Place the steel cut oats and water to the Instant Pot.

2. Close the lid on the Instant Pot and press the "Porridge" button to cook for about 6 minutes.

3. Turn the knob on the top of the lid to sealing position.

4. After about 10 minutes, the timer will automatically set to 6 minutes.

5. When the time is up, allow it to sit for an additional 6-8 minutes to release the pressure.

6. Remove the lid once the pressure has been released.

7. In a bowl, add the oatmeal and add the toppings of desired choice.

8. Serve immediately or store in an airtight container in the fridge for about 5-6 days.

Creamy Pumpkin Maple Oats

Serving Size: 4

Ingredients:

- 1 cup of gluten-free steel cut oats
- 1 13.5 ounces of can coconut milk
- 1 ¼ cups of water
- ½ tsp. of salt
- 1 tsp. of vanilla
- ¼ cup of pumpkin
- 2-3 tbsp. of maple syrup
- 1 tbsp. of brown sugar or coconut sugar
- ¼ tsp. of cinnamon
- Toasted, chopped pecans, optional

Cooking Instructions:

1. In a 6-quart Instant Pot, add the oats, coconut milk, water, salt and vanilla.

2. Close and lock the lid in place.

3. Press Manual High Pressure and set to cook for about for 10 minutes.

4. When the time is up, use a natural pressure release for about 12 minutes.

5. Stir in the pumpkin, maple syrup, brown sugar or coconut sugar and cinnamon.

6. Top with almond milk and chopped pecans.

7. Serve and enjoy!

Loaded Breakfast Potatoes

Preparation time: 10 minutes

Cook time: 20 minutes

Total time: 30 minutes

Serves: 4

Ingredients:

- 4 russet potatoes, scrubbed
- 1 pound of Butcher box pork sausage
- ¼ cup of onion, diced
- 1 red bell pepper, diced
- 1 orange bell pepper, diced
- ½ tsp. of primal palate meat & potato seasoning
- ½ tsp. of garlic powder
- A pinch of sea salt & pepper
- Handful of green onion, sliced
- Tesserae's hot buffalo sauce
- Poached eggs
- 4 eggs
- 2 tbsp. of apple cider vinegar

Cooking Instructions:

1. Pour 4 cups of water into the bottom of your Instant Pot and place the steamer rack.

2. Add the potatoes on the rack. Close and lock the lid in place.

3. Set the valve to sealing position. Select Manual High Pressure and cook the potatoes for about 20 minutes.

4. Generously spray a cast iron skillet with non-stick cooking spray. Sauté the onions until slightly translucent.

5. Add the pork sausage and use a fork to break up the sausage until it's evenly browned.

6. Add the meat, potatoes seasoning, garlic powder, salt and pepper to taste.

7. Sauté the contents together for about 2 minutes or until the peppers are tender.

8. Drain the potatoes and allow to cool before cutting into them. Use a fork to lightly scrape the sides of the potato.

9. Use a slotted spoon to stuff the inside of the potato with the pork mixture.

10. In a small pot, place a few cups of water and bring the water to a boil.

11. Add the apple cider vinegar, crack each egg, and gently drop it into the water.

12. Turn the heat off and cover the eggs for about 5 minutes.

13. Use a slotted spoon to scoop the poached eggs out of the water and place them on top of the potatoes.

14. Drizzle with Tesserae's hot buffalo sauce and sprinkle with green onions.

15. Serve and enjoy.

Quinoa Breakfast Bowls

Preparation time: 25 minutes

Cook time: 1 minutes

Total time: 25 minutes

Servings: 6

Ingredients:

Quinoa:

- 1 ½ cups of quinoa, soaked in water for about 1 hour
- 1 (15 oz.) can coconut milk, or milk of choice
- 1 ½ cups of water
- 1 tsp. of ground cinnamon
- ¼ cup of pure maple syrup
- 2 tsp. of vanilla extract
- ¼ tsp. of salt

Optional toppings:

- Fresh fruit
- Coconut flakes
- Hemp hearts
- Non-dairy milk

Cooking Instructions:

1. Rinse and drain the soaked quinoa.

2. In a bowl to be placed in your Instant Pot, place the quinoa, coconut milk, water, cinnamon, maple syrup, vanilla and salt.

3. Close and lock the lid in place. Set the lid to the sealing position and press the button for the "rice" setting.

4. Set to cook at Low pressure for about 12 minutes. When the time is up, use a natural pressure release for about 10 minutes.

5. Open the lid and divide the quinoa into 6 individual containers with lids.

6. Store the quinoa in the fridge until ready to serve.

7. Top with the non-dairy milk, fresh fruit, coconut flakes, hemp hearts when you are ready to serve and enjoy.

CHAPTER 2: SOUPS & STEWS

Minestrone Soup

Preparation time: 12 minutes

Cooking time: 6 minutes

Total time: 18 minutes

Serves: 5 to 6

Ingredients:

- 2 tablespoons of olive oil
- 2 stalks celery diced
- 1 large onion diced
- 1 large carrot diced
- 3 cloves of garlic minced
- 1 teaspoon of dried oregano
- 1 teaspoon of dried basil
- pepper to taste
- 28 ounces of san Marzano tomatoes
- 15 ounces can or about 2 cups freshly cooked, drained white or cannellini beans
- 4 cups of bone broth or vegetable broth
- 1 bay leaf
- ½ cup of fresh spinach or kale without the rib torn into shreds
- 1 cup of gluten-free elbow pasta
- 1/3 cup of finely grated parmesan cheese omit for vegan option
- 1-2 tablespoons of fresh pesto optional

Cooking Instructions:

1. Select the Sauté function on your Instant Pot, add in olive oil, onion, carrot, celery and garlic. Mix until softened.

2. Add in basil, oregano, salt and pepper. If canned tomatoes are still whole, pulse tomatoes and liquid in can in a blender or food processor for a few seconds to dice tomatoes.

3. Add tomatoes, bone broth, spinach or kale, bay leaf, and pasta. Secure the Lid, select the Manual function, cook on High Pressure for about 6 minutes.

4. When the time is up, allow it to release pressure naturally for about 1 to 2 minutes. Then do a quick pressure release.

5. Remove Lid carefully and add white kidney beans. Serve in bowls and garnish with parmesan cheese and a dollop of pesto.

6. Serve and enjoy!

Vegetable Beef Soup

Ingredients:

- 2 pounds of lean ground beef
- 1 large onion, diced
- 2 teaspoons of garlic, minced
- 1 can (14.5 ounces) stewed tomatoes, with liquid
- 3 cups of beef broth
- 4 carrots, sliced into round disks
- 3 stalks of celery, sliced or diced
- 3-4 medium-large potatoes, cut into bite-sized chunks
- 3 tablespoon of tomato paste
- ½ teaspoon of salt
- ½ teaspoon of pepper
- 2 teaspoons of dried parsley flakes
- ½ teaspoon of ground oregano

Cooking Instructions:

1. Press the sauté function on your Instant Pot.

2. Add the ground beef, onion, and garlic and sauté until the beef is cooked through.

3. Drain the excess oil and add the can of stewed tomatoes with liquid, breaking up the tomatoes into small pieces.

4. Stir in beef broth, diced vegetables, tomato paste, and seasonings.

5. Close and lock the lid in place and ensure that the vent is set to the sealing position.

6. Select Manual High Pressure and set to cook for about 4 minutes.

7. When the time is up, Press the Cancel function and turn the valve to venting position.

8. Carefully remove the lid when cooled.

9. Serve and enjoy.

Beef and Porcini Mushroom Stew

Preparation time: 5 minutes

Cook time: 20 minutes

Total time: 25 minutes

Ingredients:

- 1 tbsp. of olive oil
- 2 lbs. (1k) of beef chuck, cut into 1-inch cubes
- 1 sprig of rosemary, de-stemmed and finely chopped, 1 teaspoon
- 1 medium red onion, roughly diced
- 1 celery stalk, cut into ½-inch slices
- ½ cup (125ml) red wine
- 1 cup (250ml) of salt-free beef stock
- 1 tsp. of salt
- ¼ tsp. of pepper
- 1 oz. (30 grams) of dried porcini mushrooms, rinsed
- 2 large carrots, sliced into ½-inch rounds
- 2 tbsp. of unsalted butter
- 2 tbsp. of all-purpose flour

Cooking Instructions:

1. Press the Sauté mode and add the olive oil. Sear the beef cubes on one side for about 5 minutes.

2. Add the rosemary, onions, celery, red wine, stock, salt, and pepper to taste. Give everything a good mix in the Instant Pot. Sprinkle the mushrooms and carrots on top of the stew mixture.

3. Close and lock the lid in place and set the valve to the sealing position. Cook at High Pressure for about 20 minutes. In a small pan, add the butter to melt and drizzle with flour.

4. Mix into a paste and allow it to cook until the butter begins to make bubbles in the flour. When the timer beeps, use a natural pressure release. Add 6 tbsp. of cooking liquid from the Instant Pot into the small pan with the flour paste.

5. Mix everything very well to loosen the paste. Pour the mixture back into the pot and bring the contents to a boil using the sauté function. Allow to simmer until thickened for about 5 minutes.

6. Serve and enjoy!

Pot Borscht (Beet Soup)

Preparation time: 15 minutes

Cooking time: 15 minutes

Total time: 30 minutes

Serves: 3 to 4

Ingredients:

- 1 medium white onion, chopped
- 1 tsp. of salt
- 2 tbsp. of olive oil
- 2 large white potatoes, peeled and diced into small cubes (about 1lb / 450 g)
- 1 large carrot, grated (about 4.5 oz./ 125 g)
- 2 medium beets or 3 small ones, grated (7-8 oz. / 200-250 g)
- ¼ medium white cabbage, thinly sliced (12 oz. / 350 g)
- 4 medium cloves of garlic, diced
- 10-12 g dried porcini mushrooms
- 3 tbsp. of apple cider vinegar
- 1.5 tbsp. of tomato paste
- 1 cube beef stock
- 1 cube vegetable stock
- ½ tsp. of pepper
- 1.25 litres filtered water (5 cups)
- Fresh parsley and sour cream/yoghurt to serve

Cooking Instructions:

1. Select the Sauté function on your Instant Pot. Add the olive oil and onions and Sauté for about 2 minutes, until softened.

2. Add potatoes, carrots and beets, and give everything a good stir. Add the cabbage, garlic and the rest of the ingredients.

3. Stir through and Select the Keep Warm/Cancel button. Secure the Lid, ensure that the valve is on the sealing position.

4. Select the Manual function, cook on High Pressure for about 10 minutes. When the time is up, allow it to release pressure naturally for about 5 minutes.

5. Then use the quick release to get rid of the remaining pressure. Serve the soup with chopped fresh parsley and a dollop of sour cream. Enjoy.

Ground Beef and Potato Soup

Preparation time: 10 minutes

Cook time: 10 minutes

Total time: 20 minutes

Servings: 4

Ingredients:

- 1 pound of ground beef grass fed
- 1 cup of onion, chopped
- 3 carrots, sliced
- 2 stalks celery, chopped
- 1 ½ cups of red potatoes, sweet potato or cauliflower diced
- ½ teaspoon of oregano
- 1 teaspoon of sea salt
- 1 tablespoon of butter or ghee
- 4 cup of broth bone, beef or vegetable

Cooking Instructions:

1. Press the sauté function on your Instant Pot.

2. Add the butter/ghee, onion and ground beef.

3. Sauté the contents until the beef has evenly browned and the onions are translucent.

4. Select the Cancel/Keep Warm function. Add the broth, vegetables and seasonings.

5. Close and lock the lid in place. Select the soup button and set to cook for about 10 minutes.

6. When the time is up, use a natural pressure release for about 5 minutes.

7. Serve and enjoy!

Chicken Noodle Soup

Preparation time: 20 minutes

Cooking time: 20 minutes

Total time 40 minutes

Serves: 5 to 6

Ingredients:

- 4 whole chicken legs including thighs
- Olive oil
- 4 carrots peeled and sliced
- 4 stalks celery sliced, including leaves
- 1 onion diced
- 3 cloves garlic minced
- 6 to 8 cups chicken stock
- 1 tsp. of ground turmeric
- 1 tbsp. of soy sauce
- 1 tbsp. of ginger grated
- 8 ounces of dried rice noodles
- 4 tbsp. of minced fresh parsley

Cooking Instructions:

1. Take the chicken out of the fridge and allow it sit at room temperature for about 20 minutes, salt and pepper the chicken, prepare the veggies.

2. Select the Sauté function on your Instant Pot and add a few swirls of olive oil. Add the chicken skin side down to the pan.

3. Allow the chicken to rest undisturbed for about 5 minutes to brown, turn and brown the other side.

4. Remove the chicken. If needed, add a bit more oil to the pot. Then add in the carrots, celery, onions and garlic to the pot and sauté until slightly softened.

5. Add the turmeric, soy sauce and grated ginger and about a cup of the stock. Stir and scrap up any brown bits on the bottom.

6. Top with the chicken and pour over the remaining stock. Secure the Lid, ensure that the valve is on sealing position.

7. Select the Manual function, cook for about 12 minutes. When the time is up, do a quick pressure release.

8. Remove the chicken and set aside to cool. Turn off your Instant Pot and select the sauté function on your Instant Pot.

9. When the soup comes up to a boil, add the noodles and cook for about 5 minutes. While the noodles are cooking, separate the chicken meat from the bones.

10. When the noodles are done, turn off the Instant Pot, and stir back in the chicken. Serve topped with the fresh parsley.

11. Serve and enjoy!

Italian Sausage Stew

Ingredients:

- 2 tablespoons of butter
- ½ pound of pastured ground pork
- ½ teaspoon of onion powder
- ½ teaspoon of garlic powder
- 1½ teaspoon of basil
- ½ teaspoon of thyme
- ¼ teaspoon of cumin
- ½ teaspoon of marjoram
- ¼ teaspoon of cayenne
- 1 teaspoon of sea salt
- ¼ teaspoon of black pepper
- 1 medium onion, diced
- 2 carrots, diced
- 2 stalks of celery, diced
- 4 cloves of garlic, minced
- ½ cup of white wine
- 1 – 15 ounces of can organic diced tomatoes
- 2 quarts bone broth
- 2-3 large handfuls kale, chopped
- 8oz gluten free noodles
- Sea salt/pepper to taste
- Freshly grated parm or other raw cheese, for garnishing

Cooking Instructions:

1. Press the "Sauté" button. Once the pot is hot, add the butter to melt.

2. Add the pork and all of the seasonings. Give everything a good stir to combine and brown the meat.

3. Add the onion, carrot, celery, and garlic, combine and cook for about 5 to 7 minutes until the veggies are soft.

4. Deglaze the pan by adding the white wine and scrape up any bits at the bottom.

5. Add the diced tomatoes, broth, kale and noodles and give everything a good stir to combine.

6. Close and lock the lid in place and ensure that the valve is set to the sealing position.

7. Select Manual button to cook at High Pressure for about 3 minutes. When the time is up, use a natural pressure release.

8. Season with salt and pepper to taste. Serve with freshly grated parmesan and enjoy.

Chicken Meatball and Kale Soup

Preparation time: 10 minutes

Cooking time: 20 minutes

Total time: 30 minutes

Serves: 5 to 6

Ingredients:

For the meatballs:

- 1 ½ pounds of ground chicken breast
- 2 tablespoons of arrowroot powder or ¼ cup panko breadcrumbs
- 1 teaspoon of salt
- 1 teaspoon of pepper
- ½ teaspoon of crushed red pepper (optional)
- 1 teaspoon of garlic powder
- 1 teaspoon of onion powder
- ½ tablespoon of dried oregano
- ½ tablespoon of basil
- 2 tablespoons of nutritional yeast or grated Parmesan cheese

For soup:

- 6 cups of low sodium vegetable stock
- 4 celery stalks, diced
- 2 medium onions, diced
- 3 medium carrots, peeled and diced
- 1 bunch kale, coarsely chopped
- 2 teaspoons of thyme
- 2 garlic cloves, minced
- 2 teaspoons of salt (or to taste)
- ½ teaspoon of crushed red pepper (or to taste)
- 2 tablespoons of olive oil
- 2 eggs, beaten (opt)

Cooking Instructions:

1. Select the High Sauté function on your Instant Pot and add olive oil and heat for about 1 minute.

2. Add celery, onions, and carrots. Sauté for about 3 minutes, until vegetables start to become soft.

3. Add in garlic, salt, thyme, and red pepper. Add in kale and give everything a good stir to combine. Add the vegetable stock and continue to cook.

4. In a large bowl, combine all the ingredients for the meatballs and give everything a good mix.

5. Use a tbsp. to measure out meatballs. Wet hands to help create smooth balls and roll chicken mixture into meatballs.

6. Wet your hands, if you feel the chicken sticking to your hands. Add chicken to the soup by gently dropping into the cooking soup. (Do not stir) or the meatballs will break apart.

7. Cancel the sauté function using the cancel/keep warm button. Secure the Lid, select the Manual function, cook on High Pressure for about 15 minutes.

8. When the time is up, do a quick pressure release and return the soup to the sauté setting.

9. Slowly drizzle in beaten eggs in a circular motion throughout the pot and cook for about 2 minutes or until egg are set.

10. Turn off your Instant Pot. Serve with grated parmesan if desired.

11. Serve and enjoy!

Chicken-Sweet Potato Stew

Ingredients:

- 2 cloves grated garlic
- 1 tablespoon of grape seed oil
- 1 Star anise
- 3 cloves
- 2 bay leaves
- 1 stick of cinnamon
- 2 green chilies, slit
- 1 teaspoon of whole peppercorns
- 3 cardamom pods
- 2 pounds of chicken
- 1 large sweet potato, cubed
- 1 medium red onion, finely sliced
- 1 tomato, finely chopped
- 2 cups water
- Salt to taste
- A pinch of sugar, optional
- 1 teaspoon of butter or ghee

Cooking Instructions:

1. Add the oil in the bottom of your Instant Pot.

2. Add the garlic, all the whole spices and sauté.

3. Add the onions and tomatoes and green chilies and sauté until the onions turns translucent.

4. Add the chicken pieces and cook until it has cooked through. Add the water, cover and allow it to simmer until the chicken and potatoes are cooked.

5. Select the 'Poultry' button. Once hot, add salt and pinch of sugar.

6. Add 1 teaspoon of organic ghee or butter towards the end.

7. Serve and enjoy!

Paleo Hamburger Soup

Preparation time: 10 minutes

Cooking time: 30 minutes

Total time: 40 minutes

Serves: 3 to 4

Ingredients:

- 2 tbsp. of avocado oil
- 1 onion, diced
- 1 lb. of grass-fed ground beef
- 2 cups of chopped carrots
- 2 tbsp. of primal palate meat + potatoes seasoning
- 1 tsp. of sea salt
- 1 tbsp. of garlic powder
- 4 cups of beef broth (organic store bought or homemade)
- 5 medium Yukon gold potatoes (whole)

Cooking Instructions:

1. Select the Sauté function on your Instant Pot drizzle in the avocado oil and onion.

2. Allow the onions to cook for about 5 to 8 minutes, stirring them around so that they do not burn.

3. Add the ground beef and break it up a bit with a spatula, pour in the broth, add the seasonings and carrots and whole potatoes.

4. Close and lock the Lid in place, select the Keep Warm/Cancel button. Now select the Soup button and close the pressure valve.

5. Once it's done cooking, do a quick pressure release. Open the lid carefully and use a potato masher to break up the potatoes until they are made into small chunks

6. Serve and enjoy!

Tuscan Chicken Stew

Preparation time: 20 minutes

Cook time: 6 minutes

Total time: 26 minutes

Servings: 6

Calories: 280 kcal

Ingredients:

- 6-8 boneless chicken thighs, fat removed and cut into 1-2-inch cubes
- 2 carrots, peeled and sliced
- 2 stalks of celery, sliced
- 1 small-medium onion, diced
- 2 cloves garlic, minced
- 2 medium tomatoes, diced
- 12 baby potatoes, left whole or cut in half
- 1 ¾ cup of chicken stock
- 1 tbsp. of tomato paste, optional
- 2 tbsp. of white wine
- 1 tsp. of fennel seeds crushed with side of knife
- ½ tsp. of salt
- A sprig of fresh rosemary, roughly chopped
- ¼ cup of water
- 1 tbsp. of cornstarch
- 1 tbsp. of balsamic vinegar
- Chopped parsley, for garnishing

Cooking Instructions:

1. Press the sauté button and add 1 tablespoon of olive oil. Add the carrots, celery, onion and cook for about 5 minutes.

2. Add the chicken thighs and cook for additional 5 minutes or until lightly browned.

3. Add the garlic and cook for 1 minute. Press Cancel to turn off the sauté function.

4. Add all the remaining ingredients into the Instant Pot except for the water, cornstarch & balsamic vinegar.

5. Give everything a good stir. Cook on High Pressure for about 6 minutes.

6. When the time is up, use a natural pressure release for about 10 minutes.

7. Stir together the cornstarch and water, add with the balsamic vinegar to the stew. The stew will thicken immediately.

8. Serve and enjoy!

French Onion Soup

Preparation time: 5 minutes

Cook time: 15 minutes

Total time: 20 minutes

Serves: 4

Ingredients:

- 4 large onions, thinly sliced
- 3 tbsp. of butter
- 1 tbsp. of olive oil
- 5 cups of vegetable stock
- 2 bay leaves
- 1 tsp. of dried thyme
- 1 tsp. of salt
- 1 tsp. of black pepper
- 4 thick slices of French bread
- 4 slices Gruyere cheese

Cooking Instructions:

1. Press the sauté button and add the butter and olive oil.

2. Sauté the onions stirring frequently. Once the onions have browned, add the vegetable stock to Instant Pot.

3. Scrape the bottom of the Instant Pot and add the bay leaves, thyme, salt and pepper to taste.

4. Close and lock the lid in place. Select Manual setting and set the timer for 10 minutes.

5. When the time is up, use a natural pressure release. Turn on the oven broiler on and toast the French bread slices.

6. Spray the oven-proof soup bowl with non-stick cooking spray and add a slice of French bread toast to bottom.

7. Ladle the soup, with plenty of onions on top of bread. Add Gruyere cheese and broil until the cheese has browned and melted.

8. Serve and enjoy!

Italian Sausage Stew

Ingredients:

- 2 tablespoons of butter
- ½ pound of pastured ground pork
- ½ teaspoon of onion powder
- ½ teaspoon of garlic powder
- 1½ teaspoon of basil
- ½ teaspoon of thyme
- ¼ teaspoon of cumin
- ½ teaspoon of marjoram
- ¼ teaspoon of cayenne
- 1 teaspoon of sea salt
- ¼ teaspoon of black pepper
- 1 medium onion, diced
- 2 carrots, diced
- 2 stalks of celery, diced
- 4 cloves of garlic, minced
- ½ cup of white wine
- 1 – 15 ounces of can organic diced tomatoes
- 2 quarts bone broth
- 2-3 large handfuls kale, chopped
- 8oz gluten free noodles
- Sea salt/pepper to taste
- Freshly grated parm or other raw cheese, for garnishing

Cooking Instructions:

1. Press the "Sauté" button. Once the pot is hot, add the butter to melt.

2. Add the pork and all of the seasonings. Give everything a good stir to combine and brown the meat.

3. Add the onion, carrot, celery, and garlic, combine and cook for about 5 to 7 minutes until the veggies are soft.

4. Deglaze the pan by adding the white wine and scrape up any bits at the bottom.

5. Add the diced tomatoes, broth, kale and noodles and give everything a good stir to combine.

6. Close and lock the lid in place and ensure that the valve is set to the sealing position.

7. Select Manual button to cook at High Pressure for about 3 minutes. When the time is up, use a natural pressure release.

8. Season with salt and pepper to taste. Serve with freshly grated parmesan and enjoy.

Taco Soup

Serves: 4 servings

Preparation time: 15 minutes

Cooking time: 25 minutes

Total time: 40 minutes

Ingredients:

- 1 pound of ground beef
- 15 ounces of can black beans, drained and rinsed
- 15 ounces of can diced tomatoes, undrained
- 15 ounces of can corn, drained
- 2 tablespoon of chili powder
- 1 teaspoon of ground cumin
- 1 teaspoon of garlic powder
- 1 teaspoon of onion powder
- 2 cups of chicken or beef broth
- 1 cup hot water, if cooking frozen
- Salt and pepper to taste
- ½ cup of shredded cheese
- Crushed tortilla chips, optional for topping
- Fresh veggies, as side dish

Cooking Instructions:

1. In a large saucepan, brown and drain the ground beef.

2. Add the browned ground beef to the Instant Pot. Press the sauté button on the Instant Pot and brown the ground beef.

3. Pull the pre-browned ground beef from the freezer and add frozen to the pot. Add the black beans, corn, diced tomatoes, and chicken broth.

4. Stir in the chili powder, ground cumin, garlic powder, onion powder and hot water in with the remaining ingredients.

5. Close and lock the lid in place. Cook on Manual High Pressure for about 15 minutes. When the time is up, use a quick pressure release.

6. Prepare the fresh veggies. Top with crushed tortilla chips and cheese as garnish, with a side of veggies and enjoy.

Chicken-Sweet Potato Stew

Ingredients:

- 2 cloves grated garlic
- 1 tablespoon of grape seed oil
- 1 Star anise
- 3 cloves
- 2 bay leaves
- 1 stick of cinnamon
- 2 green chilies, slit
- 1 teaspoon of whole peppercorns
- 3 cardamom pods
- 2 pounds of chicken
- 1 large sweet potato, cubed
- 1 medium red onion, finely sliced
- 1 tomato, finely chopped
- 2 cups water
- Salt to taste
- A pinch of sugar, optional
- 1 teaspoon of butter or ghee

Cooking Instructions:

1. Add the oil in the bottom of your Instant Pot.

2. Add the garlic, all the whole spices and sauté.

3. Add the onions and tomatoes and green chilies and sauté until the onions turns translucent.

4. Add the chicken pieces and cook until it has cooked through. Add the water, cover and allow it to simmer until the chicken and potatoes are cooked.

5. Select the 'Poultry' button. Once hot, add salt and pinch of sugar.

6. Add 1 teaspoon of organic ghee or butter towards the end.

7. Serve and enjoy!

Unstuffed Cabbage Roll Soup

Servings: 9

Ingredients:

- ½ of a small onion, diced
- 2 garlic cloves, minced
- 1 ½ pound 80/20 ground beef
- 3 cups of beef broth
- 1 14 ounces of can diced tomatoes
- 1 8 ounces of can tomato sauce
- ¼ cup of Bragg's Amino
- 1 small/medium cabbage, chopped
- 3 teaspoons of Worcestershire sauce
- ½ teaspoon of parsley
- ½ teaspoon of salt
- ½ teaspoon of pepper

Cooking Instructions:

1. Press the Sauté on your Instant Pot.
2. Brown the ground beef with diced onions and garlic then drain.
3. Add the beef mixture back to the Instant Pot add all the remaining ingredients.
4. Close and lock the lid in place and ensure that the valve is set to the sealing position.
5. Turn off the Sauté function by pressing the Cancel button.
6. Press the Soup button and allow the Instant Pot to complete the soup cycle.
7. When the time is up, do a quick release of the steam valve.
8. Serve and enjoy.

CHAPTER 3: EGGS

French "Baked" Eggs

Preparation time: 6 mins

Cooking time: 8 mins

Total time: 14 mins

Ingredients:

- 4 eggs
- 4 slices of meat, fish or vegetables
- 4 slices of cheese, or shot of cream
- 4 garnish of fresh herbs
- Olive oil

Cooking Instructions:

1. Add 1 cup of water on the trivet of your pressure cooker and set aside.

2. Prepare the ramekins by adding a drop of olive oil in each and rubbing the bottom and sides.

3. After rubbing the olive oil, lay a slice of preferred meat or vegetable.

4. Break an egg and drop it into the ramekin. Then, put sliced cheese, or cream, of your choice.

5. For a soft egg yolk, cover properly with tin foil to prevent the extra hot steam from having direct contact with the egg for a hard fully-cooked yolk leave uncovered.

6. Place the ramekins in the steamer basket and lower into pressure cooker. Close and lock the Lid in place.

7. Set the pressure level to Low pressure. Then, turn the heat up high and when the pan reaches pressure, lower the heat and count about 4 minutes cooking time at Low pressure.

8. When the timer beeps, do a quick pressure release. Remove the ramekins carefully.

9. Serve immediately and enjoy!

Bacon and Egg Risotto

Preparation time: 10 minutes

Cook time: 10 minutes

Total time: 20 minutes

Serves: 2

Ingredients:

- 3 slices of center cut bacon, chopped
- 1/3 cup chopped onion
- ¾ cup arborio rice
- 3 tbsp of dry white wine
- 1 ½ cups of chicken broth
- 2 eggs
- 2 tbsp of grated parmesan cheese
- salt and pepper, to taste
- chives, for garnish

Cooking Instructions:

1. Select the sauté function on your pressure cooker and add the bacon.

2. Keep cooking until fat starts to render and bacon is crisping, about 5 minutes. Stir in the onion and cook 2 to 3 minutes more.

3. Then, stir in the rice and sauté for 1 minute. Pour in the wine and stir, scraping up any bits from the bottom of the pan.

4. When the wine has been absorbed, pour in the chicken broth and stir thoroughly. Then, close and lock the lid in place.

5. Ensure that the valve is in sealing position, then select the Manual function to cook on High Pressure for about 5 minutes.

6. When the rice has been brought to pressure, cook the eggs to your liking.

7. Once the rice is done cooking, do a quick pressure release and remove the Lid carefully.

8. Stir in the Parmesan, pepper and salt. Then, divide between two plates, add the cooked egg, and sprinkle with chives.

9. Serve immediately and enjoy!

Poached Egg in Bell Pepper Cup

Preparation time: 5 minutes

Cook time: 10 minutes

Total time: 15 minutes

Ingredients:

- 2 slices of whole wheat bread, toasted
- 2 slices of smoked Scamorza, Mozzarella or Gouda
- 1 small bunch of Rucola
- 2 fresh eggs, refrigerated
- 2 bell peppers, ends cut off

For the Mock Hollandaise sauce:

- 1½ tsp. of Dijon mustard
- 3 tbsp. of orange juice
- 1 tsp. of fresh lemon juice
- 1 tbsp. of white wine vinegar
- ½ tsp. of salt
- 1 tsp. of Turmeric

Cooking Instructions:

1. Prepare the mock Hollandaise sauce by whisking together all of the ingredients until smooth.

2. You may refrigerate overnight to be used the next day. Add 1 cup of water and steamer basket and set aside.

3. Cut the bell pepper ends to form "cups" that are about 1.5" or 4cm high, and then break an egg inside of the cup.

4. Cover with tin foil and place in the steamer basket of the Instant Pot. Close and lock the lid in place and ensure that the steam valve is set to the sealing position.

5. Select the "low" pressure setting and once the pan reaches pressure, count 3-4 minutes cooking time at low pressure.

6. When the time is up, use a natural pressure release for about 10 minutes. Stack the toast, smoked cheese, Rucola, and pepper cups and cover with a dollop of mock-Hollandaise.

7. Serve and enjoy.

Eggs En Cocotte

Preparation time: 2 minutes

Cooking time: 2 minutes

Total time: 4 minutes

Servings: 3

Ingredients:

- Butter
- 3 tbsp. of cream
- 3 fresh pasture raised eggs
- 1 tbsp. of chives
- Sea salt and freshly ground pepper
- 1 cup of water

Cooking Instructions:

1. Wipe the sides and bottoms of the ramekins with butter.

2. Pour 1 tbsp. of cream into each ramekin. Crack an egg into each ramekin and sprinkle with chives.

3. Carefully place the rack in the bottom of your Instant Pot and pour 1 cup of water.

4. Place the ramekins on rack. Close and lock the lid in place and ensure that the steam valve is in sealing position.

5. Press Manual function and set to cook at Low Pressure for about 2 minutes.

6. When the time is up, use a natural pressure release.

7. Carefully remove the lid and season with sea salt and pepper to taste.

8. Serve and enjoy.

Mexican Egg Casserole

Preparation time: 10 minutes

Cooking time: 25 minutes

Total time: 35 minutes

Serves: 7 to 8

Ingredients:

- 8 large eggs, well-beaten
- 1 lb. of mild ground sausage
- ½ large red onion, chopped
- 1 red bell pepper, chopped
- 1 can of black beans, rinsed
- ½ cup green onions
- ½ cup flour
- 1 cup of cotija cheese
- 1 cup of mozzarella cheese
- Sour cream, cilantro to garnish (optional)

Cooking Instructions:

1. Select the sauté function on your pressure cooker.

2. Once it is hot, add the sausage and onion. Cook until the sausage is cooked through, for about 6-minutes.

3. Then, mix flour with eggs until well combined. Add the egg mixture to the sausage and onions in your pressure cooker.

4. Add the chopped vegetables, beans and cheeses. You can leave a little bit of the mozzarella cheese and put that on top of the casserole when it is done.

5. Close and lock the Lid in place. Set the pressure cooker to high pressure and allow to cook for 20 minutes.

6. When the pressure cooker beeps, allow the pressure to release naturally then remove the Lid carefully.

7. Take the casserole out of the pressure cooker. Lift the inner pot out of the pressure cooker and then put a plate on top of the inner pot.

8. Flip it upside down so the casserole will pop out onto the plate. Then, add the remaining cheese to the top of the casserole.

9. Allow to sit for a couple of minutes until the cheese melts.

10. Serve and enjoy!

Egg Bake

Serves 3 to 4

Ingredients:

- Spray oil
- 6 eggs
- 2 cups of frozen hash browns
- ¼ cup of unsweetened almond milk
- ½ cup of fat free shredded cheddar cheese
- 1 tsp sea salt
- 1 teaspoon of pepper
- ½ onion, diced
- ½ green pepper, diced
- ½ red pepper, diced
- 1 cup of water
- Green onion garnish optional

Cooking Instructions:

1. Spray oil on your Instant Pot liner and press the sauté button.

2. Add the onion, green pepper, and red pepper and stir until tender.

3. Press the cancel function on your Instant Pot, add frozen hash browns while Instant Pot is still warm. Keep stirring until hash browns become soft.

4. After stirring, spray oil on a heatproof bowl that will fit inside your Instant Pot liner without touching the edges.

5. Add onion, pepper, and hash browns mixture into the heatproof bowl.

6. Whisk the eggs, milk, ¼ cup of fat free shredded cheddar, salt, and pepper together.

7. Pour the egg mixture into the heatproof bowl, stir until everything is coated. Pour 1 cup of water into your Instant Pot liner.

8. Place your heatproof bowl on top of your Instant Pot steamer rack and place it inside your liner with the steamer rack handles, then close and lock the Lid in place.

9. set vent to sealing, and set the Instant pot to high pressure and allow to cook for 20 minutes.

10. When time is up, do a quick pressure release. After the pressure release loosen the edges of the egg bake with a butter knife.

11. Sprinkle the remaining cheese on top and add green onions as garnish if you desire.

12. Serve and enjoy!

Western Omelet Quiche

Servings: 4 to 5

Ingredients:

- 6 large eggs (beaten)
- ½ cup half and half
- ⅛ tsp. Himalayan high mineral Salt
- 8 oz. Canadian bacon (diced)
- ¾ cup of red and green bell peppers (diced)
- 3 spring onions (thinly sliced, reserving tops for garnish)
- ¾ cup of cheddar cheese (shredded)
- ¼ cup of cheddar cheese (shredded, for garnish, optional)

Cooking Instructions:

1. Place the steamer rack in the bottom of your Instant Pot and add 1½ cups of water.

2. Butter or spray your souffle dish, and set aside. Whisk together the eggs, milk, salt and pepper in a large mixing bowl.

3. Add your diced Canadian bacon, diced colored peppers, spring onion slices, and cheese to your prepared 1-quart soufflé dish and mix well to combine.

4. Pour egg mixture over to top of the meat and stir to combine properly. Loosely cover the souffle dish with aluminum foil.

5. Use the long-handled trivet to place the dish in the Instant Pot liner. Then, close and lock the lid in place.

6. Select Manual, high pressure and set to cook for 30 minutes. When the time is up, allow it to count for about 10 minutes.

7. Press the Cancel function to turn off, then do a quick pressure release. Open the lid carefully, then lift out the souffle dish and remove the foil.

8. Sprinkle the top of the western quiche with additional cheese if desired.

9. It will melt nicely or you can boil until lightly browned. Garnish with chopped spring onion.

10. Serve and enjoy!

Cheesy Egg Bake

Preparation time: 5 minutes

Cooking time: 20 minutes

Total time: 25 minutes

serves: 3 to 4

Ingredients:

- 6 slices bacon, chopped
- 2 cups of frozen hash browns
- 6 eggs
- ¼ cup of milk
- ½ cup of shredded cheddar cheese
- 1 tsp. of kosher salt
- ½ tsp. of pepper
- optional add-ins: onion, red pepper, spinach, mushrooms, green onions

Cooking Instructions:

1. Chop up the bacon into small pieces then sauté in your pressure cooker until crispy.

2. Add any extra veggies that you desire and sauté until tender, for about 3 minutes.

3. Add the frozen hash browns and stir until slightly thawed, for about 2 minutes.

4. Grease a heat proof container that will fit into your Pressure Cooker. we used a round metal bowl.

5. In a separate bowl, whisk the eggs, milk, shredded cheese, salt and pepper together and then add bacon and veggie mixture to the eggs.

6. Pour the egg mixture into your greased, heat proof container. Pour in 1 ½ cups of water into your pressure cooker and set the steamer rack inside.

7. Place heat proof bowl with egg mixture on top of steamer rack. Close and lock Lid in place, select Manual high pressure and set to cook for 20 minutes.

8. When the time is up, do a quick pressure release. Loosen the edges then transfer to a large plate.

9. Serve with green onions and extra shredded cheese and enjoy.

Ham & Egg Casserole

Ingredients:

- 4 medium red potatoes
- ½ onion, diced
- 1 cup of chopped ham
- 2 cups of shredded cheddar cheese
- 10 large eggs
- 1 cup of milk
- 1 tsp. of salt
- 1 tsp. of pepper

Cooking Instructions:

1. Spray the insert of your Instant Pot with nonstick cooking spray.

2. Place the eggs and milk into the insert and whisk together until well blended.

3. Place the potatoes, ham, onions, cheese, salt and pepper to taste with the eggs.

4. Give everything a good mix until it has covered with the egg mixture. Cover the insert with a foil.

5. Place the steam rack into the bottom of your Instant Pot and pour 2 cups of water.

6. Place the foil covered insert on top of the steam rack. Close and lock the lid in place and ensure that the steam valve is set to the sealing position.

7. Press Manual and set to cook at high pressure for about 25 minutes. When the time is up, use a quick pressure release.

8. Carefully open the lid and give everything a good stir.

9. Serve with your desired toppings such as sour cream, salsa, avocado, more cheese tomatoes, and enjoy!

Mini Frittatas

Preparation time: 5 minutes

Cook time: 5 minutes

Total time: 10 minutes

Serves: 6

Ingredients:

- 5 eggs
- A splash of milk, we used almond milk
- Spices such as salt and pepper
- Cheese, veggies, meats, optional mix-in

Cooking Instructions:

1. In a medium bowl, mix together the eggs, milk, and mix-ins.

2. Pour the mixture into separate baking molds such as silicone molds.

3. Carefully place the molds on rack into the bottom of your Instant Pot with 1 cup of water.

4. Select Manual function to cook at high pressure for about 5 minutes.

5. When the time is up, use a quick pressure release.

6. Serve and enjoy!

Spanish Tortilla Potato Egg Frittata, Quiche

Preparation time: 10 minutes

Cooking time: 18 minutes

Total time: 28 minutes

Serves: 4 to 5

Ingredients:

- 6 large eggs
- 4 ounces of French Fries (defrosted) (or Hash Browns or Raw Potatoes)
- 1 tbsp. of Butter melted
- ¼ cup of spanish onions, scallions or onions, diced
- ½ tsp. of sea salt, or to taste
- ¼ tsp. of freshly ground black pepper or to taste
- 1 tsp. of fox point seasoning or other seasoning
- 1 clove fresh garlic minced
- ¼ cup of milk
- 1 tsp. of tomato paste
- 4 ounces of Cheese grated
- 1.5 cups of water

Topping:

- 1 oz. of cheese If desired

Add in options:

- Green bell pepper
- Bacon
- Spinach
- Ham
- Sausage

Cooking Instructions:

1. Peel and slice the potatoes into thin strips and soak in water for about 20 minutes.

2. In a medium bowl, whisk together eggs and seasonings until very frothy.

3. Then whisk the tomato paste and milk together in a mixing cup, after mixing add it to the egg mixture.

4. Whisk the mixture well. Put garlic and onion to the egg mixture. Grease casserole dish thoroughly.

5. After greasing remove potatoes from water and dry with a paper towel. Add the raw potatoes and pour in melted butter.

6. Skip the melted butter if you are using defrosted French fries or hash browns. Pour in egg mixture and any add ins and top with cheese if using you like.

7. Add water to your Pressure Cooker and place a Steamer rack. Place uncovered casserole dish on Steamer rack.

8. Close and lock the lid and ensure that the valve is on sealing position. Select Manual function to cook on High-Pressure for about 15 to 20 minutes.

9. When the time is up, allow a 10-minute natural pressure release and then release the remaining pressure.

10. Top with grated cheese if you like and place the Lid on top of your Pressure Cooker and allow cheese to melt.

11. Serve and enjoy!

Hard-Boiled Eggs

Yield: 4 eggs

Serving size: 1 egg

Ingredients:

- 4 large eggs
- 1 cup of water

Cooking Instructions:

1. Place the rack in the bottom of your Instant Pot.
2. Pour the water in the pot and place the eggs on the rack.
3. Select Manual, High pressure and set to cook for about 5 minutes.
4. When the time is up, use a natural pressure release for about 5 minutes, then use quick release to release any remaining pressure.
5. Run the eggs under cold running water until cool enough to hold.
6. Peel right away and serve immediately.

Crustless Veggie Quiche

Preparation time: 10 minutes

Cooking time: 30 minutes

Total time: 40 minutes

Serves: 6 to 7

Ingredients:

- 8 large eggs
- ½ cup of milk
- ½ cup of flour
- ¼ teaspoon of salt and ¼ teaspoon of pepper
- herbs (optional)
- 1 large red pepper, chopped
- 1 cup of tomatoes, sliced or chopped
- 2 large green onions, chopped
- 1 ½ cups of shredded cheese (you can use mozzarella,)
- any other veggies you want to add like peppers, zucchini, etc.

Cooking Instructions:

1. Add steamer rack in the bottom of your Instant Pot. Make an aluminum foil sling and put it in the bottom of the Instant pot.

2. After putting the aluminum foil add 1 cup of water. Then whisk the eggs, milk, flour, salt and pepper together in a large bowl.

3. Add the veggies and 1 cup of cheese until it's combined. Then, pour the mixture into a bowl that will fit inside the Instant Pot bowl.

4. Cover the bowl with aluminum foil and put the bowl on top of the Steamer rack inside your Instant Pot. Close and lock the Lid in place.

5. Select Manual function to cook on High-Pressure for about 30 minutes. When the time is up, allow the Instant Pot to release pressure naturally for about 10 minutes.

6. Open the Lid carefully and lift the bowl up using the sling then take off the aluminum foil.

7. Sprinkle the top of the quiche with the remaining ½ cup cheese, replace the aluminum foil and let sit until the cheese melts for about 3 minutes.

8. Serve and enjoy!

CHAPTER 4: POULTRY

Thai Chicken Rice Bowl

Preparation time: 10 minutes

Cooking: time 10 minutes

Total time: 20 minutes

Servings: 3 to 4

Ingredients:

- 2 tbsp. of olive oil
- 4 chicken breasts (about 2 pounds)
- 1 cup of uncooked long-grain white rice
- 2 cups of broth
- 1 tbsp. of peanut butter optional
- ½ cup of sweet chili Thai sauce
- 3 tbsp. of soy sauce - to taste
- ½ tbsp. of fish sauce
- ½ tbsp. of ginger minced
- ½ tbsp. of garlic minced
- 1 tsp. of lime juice
- 1 tsp. of Sriracha or hot sauce
- Cilantro optional garnish
- Shredded zucchini optional garnish
- Shredded carrots optional garnish
- Bean sprouts optional garnish
- Peanuts optional garnish

Cooking Instructions:

1. Select the sauté function on your Instant Pot and add the olive oil.

2. Sear the chicken breasts for 2 to 3 minutes on either side to seal in their juices and transfer to a glass baking dish. Then turn off your instant pot.

3. In a medium bowl, Mix the sweet chili Thai sauce, ginger, soy sauce, fish sauce, ginger, lime juice, sriracha (and peanut butter if you like) together.

4. Pour the sauce over the chicken breasts and stir to combine properly. Then place the rice in the Instant Pot and add the chicken and sauce over the top.

5. Add the broth and close the Lid. Select Manual function to cook on High-Pressure for about 10 minutes.

6. When time is up, allow the Instant Pot to release pressure naturally.

7. Shred the chicken with two forks and then mix with the rice before serving.

8. Garnish with cilantro, shredded veggies and peanuts if you desire.

9. Serve with extra soy sauce and enjoy.

Chicken Taco Bowls

Servings: 6 -8 servings

Ingredients:

- 4-5 uncooked boneless, skinless breasts, cut in half
- 1-2 packets taco seasoning 1 for mild flavor
- 1 15 ounces can black beans, drained and rinsed
- 1 12 ounces bag frozen corn
- 1 15.5 ounces jar salsa
- 3 cups of uncooked jasmine rice rinsed
- 3 cups of water or chicken broth
- Cheddar cheese
- Cilantro, optional
- Sour cream, optional

Cooking Instructions:

1. Add 1 cup of water or broth to the bottom of your Instant Pot.

2. Add the chicken breasts on top of the liquid. Sprinkle with taco seasoning and top with the beans and corn.

3. Pour the salsa over the top of everything. Add the rice and the remaining water or broth.

4. Select Manual and set to cook at high pressure for about 12 minutes.

5. When the time is up, use a quick pressure release to release the pressure.

6. Carefully open the lid and shred the chicken with two forks.

7. Serve topped with cheddar cheese, cilantro, and sour cream if desired.

Orange Chicken

Preparation time: 5 minutes

Cook time: 15 minutes

Total time: 20 minutes

Ingredients:

- 4 chicken breasts
- ¾ cup of favorite dark sweet barbecue sauce, we used sweet baby ray's
- 2 tablespoon of soy sauce
- ¾ cup of orange marmalade
- 1 teaspoon of cornstarch
- Chopped green onions, for garnish

Cooking Instructions:

1. First, chop the chicken breasts into hearty bite size chunks.

2. Add the chopped chicken, barbecue sauce, and soy sauce in the bottom of your Instant Pot.

3. Cook on manual high pressure for about 4 minutes. When the time is up, use a quick pressure release.

4. In a medium bowl, scoop out ¼ cup of the barbecue chicken sauce and mix with cornstarch.

5. Add the cornstarch broth mixture back into the Instant Pot and add the orange marmalade.

6. Give everything a good mix. Press the sauté function and sauté for about 6 minutes or until the sauce thickens.

7. Let it to rest for about 5 minutes before serving. Garnish with green onions.

8. Serve over rice or noodles and enjoy.

Creamy Chicken Noodle Soup

Preparation time: 10 minutes

Cooking time: 10 minutes

Total time: 20 minutes

Serves: 3 to 4

Ingredients:

- 3 large carrots, peeled and sliced
- 2 stalks of celery, sliced
- 1 cup of chopped spinach
- 1 boneless skinless chicken breast chopped (fresh or frozen)
- 1 tsp. of parsley
- 1 tsp. of salt
- ½ tsp. of thyme
- ¼ tsp. of garlic powder
- 1/8 tsp. of black pepper
- 4 cups of low sodium chicken broth
- 1 cup of short pasta such as Ditalini or Orzo
- 1 cup 1% milk
- 2 tbsp. of corn starch

Cooking Instructions:

1. Add carrots, celery, spinach, chicken, parsley, thyme, salt, garlic powder, black pepper and chicken broth in your Instant Pot and stir well.

2. Close and lock the Lid in place and ensure that the valve is on sealing position. Select Manual function to cook on High-Pressure for about 4 to 5 minutes.

3. (4 minutes for veggies with more bite, 5 minutes for tender veggies). It will take about 10 minutes to come to pressure and start counting down.

4. When the time is up, turn off the Instant Pot. Do a quick pressure release and open the lid carefully.

5. Select the sauté function on your Instant Pot and add the pasta. Cook and stir for 4 to5 minutes until pasta is all dente.

6. Whisk the milk and corn starch together and stir into the soup. It will thicken as it sits and cools. Serve and enjoy.

Salsa Shredded Chicken

Serves: 5

Ingredients:

- 1 lb. of skinless, boneless chicken breast
- ½ tsp. of kosher salt
- ¾ tsp. of cumin
- Black pepper, to taste
- A pinch of oregano
- 1 cup of chunky salsa

Cooking Instructions:

1. Generously season the chicken on both sides with the spices.

2. Add the chicken into the Instant Pot and cover with salsa.

3. Close and lock the lid in place. Select Manual High Pressure to cook for about 20 minutes.

4. When the time is up, use a natural pressure release.

5. Carefully open the lid and remove the chicken onto a plate.

6. Shred the chicken with two forks.

7. Serve and enjoy!

Chili-Lime Chicken

Ingredients:

- 2 lbs. of boneless, skinless chicken breasts
- 2 medium sized limes
- 1 ½ tsp. of chili powder
- 1 tsp. of cumin
- 1 tsp. of onion powder
- 1 tsp. of kosher salt
- ¼ tsp. of black pepper
- 6 cloves garlic, finely minced or pressed
- ½ tsp. of liquid smoke

Cooking Instructions:

1. Cut the chicken breasts in half if they are more than 1-inch thick.

2. Add the chicken in bottom of your Instant Pot and squeeze in the juice of both limes.

3. Sprinkle all of the seasonings and liquid smoke over chicken.

4. Add the garlic and use your hands to rub the spice mixture all over the chicken.

5. Close and lock the lid in place and ensure that the valve is set in sealing position. Cook at high pressure for about 6 minutes.

6. When the time is up, use a natural pressure release for about 10 minutes.

7. Use an instant-read thermometer to check the temperature of the chicken and ensure that the internal temperature is about 165 degrees.

8. Use two forks to shred the chicken and place it back to the Instant Pot and toss in juices.

9. Season with more salt and pepper to taste.

10. Serve and enjoy.

Cream Cheese Chicken Pasta

Ingredients:

- 4 to 6 boneless, skinless chicken breasts
- 1 can cream of chicken soup
- 8 ounces of package of cream cheese
- 1 package of Italian dressing dry mix
- 2 cups of chicken broth

Cooking Instructions:

1. Add the chicken breasts, broth, soup, cream cheese and dressing mix into the bottom of your Instant Pot.

2. Close and lock the lid in place and seal the steam valve.

3. Press the Poultry setting and set to cook for about 15 minutes.

4. When the time is up, use a natural pressure release for about 5 minutes, then quick release to release any remaining pressure.

5. While the Instant Pot is cooking, bring a pot of water in your stove to a boil and cook the pasta according to the directions on the package.

6. Shred the chicken with two forks and serve over the pasta.

Buffalo Chicken Lettuce Wraps

Preparation time: 10 minutes

Cooking time: 15 minutes

Total time: 25 minutes

Serves: 3 to 4

Ingredients!

- 1 large boneless skinless chicken breast (about 16-20 oz)
- 1 celery stalk (for cooking with the chicken)
- 1 medium onion, diced
- 1 clove of garlic
- 16 ounces of low sodium chicken broth
- ½ cup of buffalo wing sauce (about 6 oz)
- large lettuce leaves (Romaine or Iceberg)
- ½ cup shredded carrots
- 1 large celery stalk, thinly sliced (for topping the lettuce wraps)
- ranch dressing, for topping

Cooking Instructions!

1. Add the chicken, onions, garlic, one celery stalk, buffalo wing sauce and broth to your Instant Pot.

2. Close and lock the Lid into place, and ensure that the valve is on sealing position.

3. Select manual setting and set the timer to cook for 15 minutes.

4. When the time is up, allow the Instant Pot to release pressure naturally for about 5 minutes. Then do a quick pressure release to release the remaining pressure.

5. Shred the chicken with two forks and serve in lettuce cups topped with buffalo chicken, chopped celery, shredded carrots, and ranch.

6. Serve and enjoy!

Chicken Faux Pho

Preparation time: 15 minutes

Cooking time: 30 minutes

Total time: 45 minutes

Ingredients:

- 4 pounds of assorted chicken pieces bone-in and skin on
- 2 medium onions quartered
- 1-inch ginger, peeled and roughly chopped
- 1 tbsp. of coriander seed
- 1 tsp. of green cardamom pods
- 1 black cardamom pod
- 1 cinnamon stick
- 4 cloves
- 1 lemon grass stalk trimmed and cut into 2-inch pieces
- ¼ cup of fish sauce
- 1 cup fresh cilantro
- 1 head bok choy roughly chopped
- 1 large daikon root spiralized
- Sea salt to taste

For Garnish:

- Lime wedges
- Fresh basil
- Mung bean sprouts
- 2 jalapenos thinly sliced
- ¼ onion thinly sliced

Cooking Instructions:

1. In a dry skillet, place the coriander seeds.

2. Toast the coriander seeds over medium low heat until it is fragrant and golden brown for about 5 to 6 minutes.

3. Rinse the chicken pieces and add them into the bottom of your Instant Pot. Add together the dry spices, cilantro, onion, lemon grass, and fish sauce.

4. Pour in sufficient cold water to cover the surface. Close and lock the lid in place and ensure that the steam valve is set in sealing position.

5. Select Manual function and set to cook at high pressure for about 30 minutes. When the time is up, use a natural pressure release.

6. Carefully open the lid and remove the chicken pieces. Shred the chicken with two forks. Strain the broth and add it back to the Instant Pot.

7. Adjust the seasoning to suit your desired taste. Bring to a simmer and add the bok choy and spiralized daikon.

8. Cook for about 5 to 6 minutes until it is tender. Divide the noodles and shredded chicken into serving plates and ladle in the broth.

9. Serve with the garnishes and enjoy!

Chipotle Chicken Black Beans and Rice

Preparation time: 10 minutes

Cooking time: 6 minutes

Total time: 16 minutes

Serves: 5 to 6

Ingredients:

- 1 lb. of Boneless Skinless Chicken Breasts or thighs, cut into bite sized pieces
- 1 small onion chopped
- 4 cups of diced tomatoes in juice
- 1 tablespoon of chipotle peppers in adobo pureed
- ½ cup of filtered water
- 1 cup of jasmine rice uncooked
- ½ lime, juiced
- 2 teaspoon of sea salt (real salt)
- ½ teaspoon of finely ground black pepper
- 2 tabspoon of butter (pasture raised, grass fed) ghee or coconut oil
- 1 can organic black beans drained & rinsed

Cooking Instructions:

1. Combine chicken, onion, tomatoes with juice, peppers, water, lime juice, rice, salt, pepper and butter in your pressure cooker.

2. Cook under pressure for 6 minutes. When time is up, do a quick pressure release.

3. After the pressure release, open and add black beans then stir to combine.

4. Season with additional salt & pepper, to taste.

5. Serve with a garnish of shredded cheese, sour cream and guacamole for a complete meal.

6. Serve and enjoy!

Chicken Breasts

Preparation time: 3 minutes

Cooking time: 20 minutes

Total time: 23 minutes

Serves: 3 to 4

Ingredients:

- 1 tbsp. of oil (we use avocado, but you can use coconut or canola)
- 3 boneless, skinless chicken breasts (uncooked)
- ¼ tsp. of garlic salt per chicken breast (you can use just garlic powder and regular salt)
- dash black pepper
- 1/8 tsp. of dried oregano
- 1/8 tsp. of dried basil
- 1 cup of water

Cooking Instructions:

1. Press the sauté function on the Instant Pot at the highest setting,

2. Add oil to the pot. Season one side of the chicken breasts.

3. After the display reads "hot," add the chicken breasts, seasoned side down, to the pot.

4. We used tongs to avoid hot oil splatter, add seasoning on the second side and cook for about 3 to 4 minutes on each side.

5. Remove it from pot with the tongs. Then add 1 cup of water to the pot (may need more for 8-quart pots), plus the steamer rack.

6. Place the chicken on the steamer rack. Close and lock the Lid in place, Select Manual function to cook on High-Pressure for about 5 minutes.

7. When time is up, allow the Instant pot to release pressure naturally for about 5 minutes. Then do a quick pressure release.

8. Remove the chicken from the pot, and allow to rest for about 5 minutes before serving.

9. Serve and enjoy!

Indian Butter Chicken

Ingredients:

- 2 pounds of chicken breast or tenderloins diced into ¼ inch pieces
- 1 stick of butter or ½ a cup
- 2 tsp. of garam masala
- 2 tsp. of cayenne pepper, optional
- 2 tsp. of curry powder
- 1 tsp. of ground cumin
- 1 tsp. of ground ginger OR 2 tsp. of minced fresh ginger
- 1 can of coconut milk in can
- 1 cup of chicken stock
- 1 6 ounces can of tomato paste
- 1 onion, minced
- 5 garlic cloves, minced
- Cilantro for garnishing
- Salt to taste
- 2 tablespoons of cornstarch
- 1 tablespoon of water

Cooking Instructions:

1. Press the sauté mode on your Instant Pot and place the stick of butter into the pot.

2. Allow the butter to melt until it becomes foamy. Toss in onions and garlic and cook until they are halfway done.

3. Add the coconut milk, chicken stock, tomato paste and mix thoroughly. Add the curry powder, ground cumin, ginger, cayenne pepper, garam masala, and salt to suit your desired taste.

4. Add the frozen or thawed chicken and cover with sauce. Select Manual High Pressure and set to cook for about 15 minutes.

5. When the time is up, use a natural pressure release for about 10 minutes. Press the Sauté button or Keep Warm Method.

6. Gently cut or shred the chicken into your desired size pieces with spoon and fork. Mix together the cornstarch and water and then add to the pot and mix thoroughly.

7. Allow the pot to boil until the sauce has thickened. Serve over a bed of basmati rice or jasmine rice. Garnish with fresh cut cilantro and enjoy!

BBQ Chicken with Potatoes

Ingredients:

- 2 pounds frozen chicken if fresh, adjust cooking time
- 1 cup favorite BBQ sauce
- ½ cup water
- 1 Tablespoon Italian seasoning
- 1 Tablespoon minced garlic
- 2-3 large potatoes, chopped
- 1 large red onion, sliced

Cooking Instructions:

1. Add all of the ingredients into the bottom of your Instant Pot.

2. Close and lock the lid in place and ensure that the valve is set in sealing position.

3. Press the Poultry setting and set to cook for about 15 minutes.

4. If cooking fresh chicken, cooking time of 12 minutes should be enough.

5. When the time is up, use a natural pressure release for about 10 minutes.

6. Carefully open the lid and remove the chicken.

7. Shred the chicken with two forks. Place the chicken back in the pot and toss until chicken is covered in sauce.

8. Serve and enjoy!

Shredded Mexican Chicken

Serves: 6

Preparation time: 5 minutes

Cook time: 37 minutes

Total time: 42 minutes

Ingredients:

- 2 pounds of boneless skinless chicken breasts
- 1 tablespoon of olive oil
- ½ cup of mild salsa
- 1-2 cans of green chilies
- 4 tablespoons of brown sugar
- 14.5 ounces of can diced tomatoes
- 1 tablespoon of chili powder
- 1 teaspoon of cumin
- 1 teaspoon of garlic
- ½ teaspoon of smoked paprika
- ½ tsp. of oregano
- 1 ½ teaspoon of salt
- 3 drops black pepper vitality essential oil OR, ½ teaspoon of black pepper
- 1 teaspoon of liquid smoke

Cooking Instructions:

1. Place the chicken on the bottom of your Instant Pot and brush with the olive oil.

2. Add all the remaining ingredients on top of the chicken.

3. Close and lock the lid in place and set the steam valve in sealing position.

4. Select Manual function to cook at high pressure for about 27 minutes.

5. When the time is up, use a natural pressure release. Carefully open the lid and remove the chicken to shred with two forks.

6. Place the chicken back in the Instant Pot and set to cook on slow cooker with the lid on for about 10 to 15 more minutes to absorb all the liquid.

7. Serve with hot sauce and enjoy!

Pulled Tandoori Chicken

Preparation time: 10 minutes

Cooking time: 35 minutes

Total time: 45 minutes

Serves: 4 to 5

Ingredients:

- 2 to 3 large boneless, skinless chicken breasts
- ½ cup of water
- 3 cloves of garlic, minced
- 1 tbsp. of extra virgin olive oil or coconut oil
- ½ onion, minced
- 1 can of full fat coconut milk
- 2 teaspoons of smoked paprika
- 1 teaspoon of turmeric
- 1 ½ teaspoons of ground cumin
- 1 ½ teaspoons of black pepper
- 1 teaspoon of cayenne pepper - optional
- 2 tablespoons of cilantro for garnish
- 1 ½ teaspoons of sea salt, or to taste

Cooking Instructions:

1. Place frozen chicken breasts in the Instant Pot with ½ cup of water.

2. Close and lock the Lid in place and ensure that the valve is on sealing position. Select Manual function to cook on High-Pressure for about 26 minutes.

3. Using thawed chicken breasts, add ½ cup of water to your Instant pot. Close and lock the Lid in place and ensure that the valve is on sealing position.

4. Select Manual function to cook on High-Pressure for about 15 minutes. When the time is up, do a quick release.

5. Drain the water and remove the chicken. On a cutting board, spend a few minutes pulling the chicken.

6. Add the oil, garlic and onion to the Instant Pot. Select the sauté function on your Instant Pot and cook the onion and garlic 2 to 3 minutes, turn the sauté function off.

7. Add the chicken back to the pot along with the coconut milk, cumin, turmeric, smoked paprika, and black pepper. Stir to combine well.

8. Add 1 ½ teaspoons of sea salt and stir to combine, add more as needed.

9. Serve immediately over rice and enjoy!

Sweet & Sour Chicken Wing

Ingredients:

- 1 pound of chicken wings, thawed
- Your favorite marinade or seasoning
- ½ soy sauce
- ½ cup of sweet and sour dipping sauce

Cooking Instructions:

1. Marinade the chicken wings with your desired dressing or marinade.

2. We used Italian dressing and marinade it overnight and left it in fridge.

3. Add the chicken wings to the bottom of your Instant pot. Add the ½ cup of your favorite marinade. Add the soy sauce.

4. Press the Manual function and set to cook at high pressure for about 10 minutes.

5. When the time is up, use a quick pressure release. Carefully open the lid.

6. Remove the cooked chicken wings on a pan. Pour the sweet and sour dipping sauce on the chicken wings.

7. Ensure that the wings are basted with this sauce. Broil them for about 7 minutes, turning them once.

8. Serve and enjoy!

Cashew Butter Chicken

Preparation time: 5 minutes

Cooking time: 4 hours

Total time: 4 hours 5 minutes

Serves: 5 to 6

Ingredients:

- 2 pounds of chicken breast large or chicken tenders
- ½ cup of smooth cashew butter
- ¼ cup of coconut aminos or GF Tamari Soy Sauce
- ¼ cup of honey
- ¼ cup of rice vinegar
- 1 tablespoon of sriracha
- ½ cup of chicken broth
- 3 cloves of garlic minced
- 1/3 cup of full fat canned coconut milk optional
- 3 tablespoons of chopped cilantro optional
- 3 tablespoons of chopped cashews optional

Cooking Instructions:

1. Cut your chicken into small chunks, and place inside your Instant pot.

2. Mix cashew butter, coconut aminos or soy sauce, honey, rice vinegar, sriracha, chicken broth, and garlic together in a small bowl.

3. Mix well to form a sauce and pour on top of the chicken. Close and lock the Lid in place, Select Manual function to cook on High-Pressure for about 7 minutes.

4. When the timer beeps, do a quick pressure release to release the remaining pressure. Shred the chicken or keep it in chunks. Stir in coconut milk (if using).

5. Serve over rice, cauliflower rice, or quinoa. Top with cashews and cilantro for garnish (if using).

6. Serve and enjoy!

Salsa Lime Chicken Tacos

Preparation time: 5 minutes

Cook time: 7 minutes

Total time: 12 minutes

Servings: 4

Ingredients:

- 2 lbs. of chicken breast boneless and skinless or 2 lbs. chicken thighs, skinless and with or without bones
- 2 tsp. of true lime garlic cilantro
- 1 tsp. of ground cumin
- 1 tsp. of sea salt to taste
- 1 tub fresh salsa
- 1-2 limes
- Rice
- 2 tablespoons of fresh cilantro leaves, chopped
- 1 teaspoon of true lime garlic cilantro
- 1 tablespoon of butter

Cooking Instructions:

1. First, remove all the fat from the chicken.

2. Sprinkle with the seasonings on each sides of the chicken.

3. Add the seasoned chicken to the Instant Pot, pour the salsa and squeeze 1 lime over the chicken. Add the cilantro lime rice.

4. Close and lock the lid in place. Cook at High Pressure for about 6 minutes.

5. When the time is up, use a natural pressure release for about 10 minutes.

6. Carefully remove the lid and squeeze more lime, if desired.

7. Shred the chicken with a fork.

8. Serve in taco shells, burritos, lettuce leaves, or on a salad and enjoy.

Buffalo Chicken Lettuce Wraps

Servings: 4

Ingredients:

- 1 large boneless skinless, chicken breast, about 16-20 ounces
- 1 celery stalk
- 1 medium onion, diced
- 1 clove garlic
- 16 ounces of low sodium chicken broth
- ½ cup of buffalo wing sauce, about 6 ounces
- large lettuce leaves, Romaine or Iceberg
- ½ cup of shredded carrots
- 1 large celery stalk, thinly sliced
- Ranch dressing, for topping

Cooking Instructions:

1. Add together the chicken, onions, one celery stalk, garlic, buffalo wing sauce and broth to the bottom of your Instant Pot.

2. Close and lock the lid in place and ensure that the valve is in sealing position.

3. Select the poultry or manual setting for about 15 minutes.

4. When the time is up, use a naturally pressure release for about 5 minutes, then quick release any remaining pressure.

5. Use two forks to shred the chicken.

6. Serve in lettuce cups topped with buffalo chicken, chopped celery, shredded carrots, and ranch.

Lemon Garlic Chicken

Ingredients:

- 1 to 2 lb. of chicken breasts or thighs
- 1 tsp. of sea salt
- 1 onion, diced
- 1 tbsp. of avocado oil, lard, or ghee
- 5 garlic cloves, minced
- ½ cup of organic chicken broth or homemade
- 1 tsp. of dried parsley
- ¼ tsp. of paprika
- ¼ cup of white cooking wine
- 1 large lemon juiced (or more to taste)
- 3 to 4 tsp. (or more) arrowroot flour

Cooking Instructions:

1. Select the sauté function on your Instant Pot and add the diced onion and cooking fat.

2. Cook the onions for 5 to 10 minutes or until (softened or start to brown).

3. Add in the remaining ingredients except for the arrowroot flour. Then close and lock the Lid in place.

4. Select Manual function to cook on High-Pressure for about 12 to 15 minutes and ensure that the valve is on sealing position.

5. When the time is up, release steam valve to vent and then carefully remove lid.

6. You may thicken your sauce by making a slurry.

7. To do this remove about ¼ cup of sauce from the pot, add in the arrowroot flour, and then reintroduce the slurry into the remaining liquid.

8. Serve immediately and enjoy!

Faux-Tesserae Chicken

Preparation time: 5 minutes

Cook time: 33 minutes

Total time: 38 minutes

Servings: 4

Ingredients:

- 2 ½ to 3 lb. whole chicken
- 2 tbsp. of olive oil, divided
- Sea salt and black pepper, to taste
- ½ medium onion, cut into quarters
- 5 large cloves fresh garlic, peeled and left whole
- 2 tbsp. of your favorite seasoning
- 1 cup chicken stock/broth, or water

Southwest Seasoning:

- 1 tsp. of garlic powder
- 1 tsp. of onion powder
- 1 tsp. of chili powder
- ½ tsp. of cumin
- ½ tsp. of basil

Cooking Instructions:

1. Rub the chicken with 1 tbsp. of olive oil and sprinkle with salt and pepper.

2. Add the onion wedges and garlic cloves inside the chicken. Secure the legs with butcher's twine.

3. Press the Sauté button and add the remaining olive oil. When hot, add the chicken and sear both sides for about 4 minutes on each side.

4. Remove the chicken and set aside. Place the trivet at the bottom of the Instant Pot and add the chicken stock.

5. Sprinkle and rub the entire chicken with the seasoning mix. Place the chicken, breast side up on top of the trivet.

6. Close and lock the lid in place and ensure that the lid is in "Sealing" position.

7. Select Manual function and set to cook at high pressure for about 25 minutes.

8. When the time is up, allow the pressure to release naturally for about 15 minutes.

9. Carefully open the lid and remove the chicken. Let the chicken to rest for about 5-10 minutes before serving.

Honey Curry Chicken

Preparation time: 5 minutes

Serves: 4 to 5

Ingredients:

- ¼ cup of unsalted butter, melted
- ½ cup of honey
- ¼ cup of yellow mustard
- 1 tsp. of salt
- 1 ½ tsp. of hot curry powder
- ¼ tsp. of cayenne pepper (adjust to taste)
- 1.5 pounds of boneless skinless chicken thighs or breasts

Cooking Instructions

1. Add butter, honey, mustard, salt, curry powder, and cayenne pepper to the pot of the pressure cooker and stir to combine well.

2. Add steamer rack to the pot and arrange chicken on steamer rack.

3. Select Manual function to cook on High-Pressure for (13 minutes for thighs or 18 minutes for breasts).

4. When the time is up, allow the pressure cooker to release pressure naturally for about 10 minutes.

5. When chicken is cooked, use two forks to transfer it to a serving dish.

6. Pull the chicken apart into pieces, cover with foil to keep warm while you finish the sauce. Remove steamer rack from cooking pot and turn on sauté function.

7. Bring to gentle boil, stirring frequently to reduce and thicken sauce, about 5 minutes. Add sauce to chicken and stir to coat.

8. Serve over steamed rice and enjoy!

Italian Chicken

Serves: 6 to 7

Ingredients:

- 1 tbsp. of olive oil
- ¾ cup of onion
- ½ cup green bell pepper
- ½ cup of red bell pepper
- ¼ teaspoon of salt
- ¾ cup of marinara
- 2 tablespoons of pesto
- 2 pounds of chicken breasts
- ¾ cup of very thinly sliced mushrooms

Cooking Instructions:

1. Select the sauté function on your Instant Pot and add the olive oil, onion, bell peppers and salt.

2. Sauté for 3 to 4 minutes or until the vegetables are softened, then add the marinara, pesto and chicken.

3. Cook thawed chicken on high pressure for 12 minutes. (Cook frozen chicken on high pressure for 20 minutes.)

4. When the time is up, do a quick pressure release.

5. Remove the chicken breasts from the pot and place on a cutting board. Use two forks to shred the chicken.

6. After shredding the chicken, remove ⅔ cup of liquid from the pot carefully to leave the vegetables. Reserve the liquid for cooking rice or making soup.

7. Add the mushrooms to the vegetables and sauté for 2 to 3 minutes until mushrooms are slightly softened.

8. Return the shredded chicken to pot and stir until well combined.

9. Serve and enjoy!

Chicken Soup

Preparation time: 5 minutes

Cook time: 40 minutes

Total time: 45 minutes

Serves: 4

Ingredients:

- Chicken broth
- 4 frozen bone-in skin-on chicken thighs
- 2 cups of chicken stock or water
- 2 slices ginger
- 4 green onions, chopped OR ½ onion, chopped

Soup ingredients:

- 4 carrots, peeled and sliced
- 2 zucchinis, peeled, seeded and sliced
- 1 lb. of mushrooms, stemmed and sliced
- Salt and black pepper to taste

Cooking Instructions:

1. Combine together the chicken, chicken stock, 2 cups of water, ginger, and green onion in the Instant Pot.

2. Select Manual to cook at High Pressure for about 30 minutes.

3. While the stock is cooking, prepare and cut the veggies.

4. Remove and discard the ginger and green onion from the soup. Add the carrot, zucchini, and mushroom to the soup.

5. Sauté the vegetables until the vegetables are cooked through.

6. Season with salt and black pepper to taste.

7. Serve warm and enjoy.

Braised Chicken Drumsticks in Tomatillo Sauce

Ingredients:

- 6 chicken drumsticks, on the bone, skin removed, about 24 ounces
- 1 tablespoon of cider vinegar
- 1 teaspoon of kosher salt
- 1/8 teaspoon of black pepper
- 1 tsp. of dried oregano
- 1 tsp. of olive oil
- 1 ½ cups of jarred tomatillo sauce
- ¼ cup of chopped cilantro, divided
- 1 jalapeno, halved and seeded

Cooking Instructions:

1. Generously season the chicken with vinegar, salt, pepper and oregano.

2. Marinate for a couple of hours.

3. Press the sauté function and add the oil when hot.

4. Add the chicken to brown evenly on both sides for about 4 minutes on each side.

5. Add the tomatillo salsa, 2 tbsp. of the cilantro and jalapeno. Close and lock the lid in place.

6. Select Manual function and set to cook at High Pressure for about 20 minutes, or until the chicken is tender.

7. When the time is up, use a natural pressure release for about 10 minutes.

8. Garnish with cilantro and serve over rice if desired.

Salsa Lime Chicken Tacos

Preparation time: 5 minutes

Cook time: 7 minutes

Total time: 12 minutes

Servings: 4

Ingredients:

- 2 lbs. of chicken breast boneless and skinless or 2 lbs. chicken thighs, skinless and with or without bones
- 2 tsp. of true lime garlic cilantro
- 1 tsp. of ground cumin
- 1 tsp. of sea salt to taste
- 1 tub fresh salsa
- 1-2 limes
- Rice
- 2 tablespoons of fresh cilantro leaves, chopped
- 1 teaspoon of true lime garlic cilantro
- 1 tablespoon of butter

Cooking Instructions:

1. First, remove all the fat from the chicken.

2. Sprinkle with the seasonings on each sides of the chicken.

3. Add the seasoned chicken to the Instant Pot, pour the salsa and squeeze 1 lime over the chicken. Add the cilantro lime rice.

4. Close and lock the lid in place. Cook at High Pressure for about 6 minutes.

5. When the time is up, use a natural pressure release for about 10 minutes.

6. Carefully remove the lid and squeeze more lime, if desired.

7. Shred the chicken with a fork.

8. Serve in taco shells, burritos, lettuce leaves, or on a salad and enjoy.

CHAPTER 5: FISH & SEAFOODS

Creamy Fish Chowder

Serves: 4 to 5

Ingredients:

- ¾ cup of chopped bacon
- 1 small/medium onion, chopped
- 2 ribs celery, chopped
- 1 medium carrot, chopped
- 2 cloves of garlic, minced or pressed
- 3 cups of Peeled & Cubed Potatoes preferably Yukon gold
- 4 cups of chicken bone-broth or vegetable broth
- 2 tbsp. of butter (pasture raised, grass fed) or ghee
- 1 lb. of wild caught Haddock FiletsFROZEN
- 1 cup of frozen or freeze-dried corn
- sea salt (real salt)
- Ground White Pepper
- 2 cups of heavy cream
- 1 heaping tbsp. of organic potato starch

Cooking Instructions:

1. Select the sauté function on your pressure cooker, cook bacon in butter until crispy.

2. Add onion, garlic, carrot and celery, cook for about 3 minutes. Season with sea salt and white pepper.

3. Add potatoes, corn, fish and broth. Cook under high pressure for 5 minutes.

4. When time is up, allow pressure cooker to release pressure naturally.

5. Combine heavy cream and potato starch, mix well. Add to chowder and Stir well.

6. Select the pressure cooker Warm function if it did not by default.

7. On the warm function, allow it to thicken slightly for about 2 to3 minutes.

8. Serve and enjoy!

Shrimp and Lentil Stew

Preparation time: 10 minutes

Cooking time: 12 minutes

Total time: 22 minutes

Serves: 5 to 6

Ingredients:

- 1 tbsp. of olive oil
- 3 cloves of garlic, minced
- 1 Onion, chopped small
- 1 red bell pepper, chopped
- 1 tbsp. of thyme
- 2 tsp. of oregano
- 2 tsp. of old Bay Seasoning
- ½ tsp. of Cayenne
- 1 cup of lentils
- 1 pound of shrimp, deveined and peeled
- 3 cups of chicken broth (or vegetable)
- 1 15 oz. can Diced Tomatoes, drain slightly
- ½ cup of tomato sauce
- 2 tbsp. of Worcestershire sauce
- 1 cup of frozen riced broccoli

Cooking Instructions:

1. Select the sauté function on your Instant Pot and add the olive oil, garlic, onion, and bell pepper and sauté for 5 minutes.

2. Add the thyme, oregano, old bay, and cayenne and toss to mix, continue to sauté for an additional 1 minute.

3. Place the lentils, shrimp, chicken broth, diced tomatoes, tomato sauce, Worcestershire sauce and riced broccoli into your Instant Pot.

4. Select Manual function to cook on High-Pressure for about 12 minutes.

5. Release the steam and season with Salt and Pepper.

6. Serve and enjoy!

Coconut Red Curry Shrimp

Preparation time: 5 minutes

Cooking time: 25 minutes

Total time: 30 minutes

Serves: 5 to 6

Ingredients:

- ¼ cup of coconut milk canned
- 1 teaspoon of cumin
- 1 teaspoon of paprika
- 2 teaspoons of curry spice
- 3 tablespoons of fresh lime juice
- ½ teaspoon of sea salt
- 1 teaspoon of freshly grated ginger
- 1 clove of garlic minced
- 2 pounds of large shrimp peeled and deveined

For Sauce:

- 2 tablespoons of coconut oil or olive oil
- 1 small white onion diced
- 2 teaspoons of freshly grated ginger
- 2 cloves of garlic minced
- 1 28 oz. can of diced tomatoes
- 3 tablespoons of red Thai curry paste
- 1 14 oz. of coconut milk
- 1 teaspoon of sea salt
- 1/3 cup of freshly chopped cilantro for garnish optional

Cooking Instructions:

1. Start by making your marinade.

2. In a medium bowl, whisk coconut milk, spices, lime juice, sea salt, ginger, and garlic together. then add shrimp.

3. Toss to coat and let sit while you are preparing the sauce. Select the sauté function on your Instant Pot, once hot then add oil to coat the bottom of the pan.

4. After coating the bottom of the pan. Add onion, ginger, and garlic. Allow to Sauté for a few minutes, then select the cancel function.

5. Add tomatoes, curry paste, coconut milk, and salt. Close and lock the Lid in place and ensure that the valve is on sealing position.

6. Select the Manual function, and cook on High Pressure for about 7 minutes. When the time is up, do a quick pressure release on your Instant Pot.

7. Remove the lid carefully, and select cancel function on your Instant Pot. Select, sauté function and add in shrimp plus juices from the marinade.

8. Simmer until the shrimp is cooked through and no longer pink for about 4 to 5 minutes.

9. Serve with optional cilantro, salt to taste, and over rice.

10. Serve and enjoy.

Fish Stew

Preparation time: 5 minutes

Cooking time: 15 minutes

Total time: 20 minutes

Serves: 3 to 4

Ingredients:

- 4 tbsp. of extra-virgin olive oil, divided
- 1 medium red onion, quartered and thinly sliced
- 4 garlic cloves, roughly chopped
- ½ cup of dry white wine
- 8 ounces of bottle clam juice (or other seafood/shellfish stock)
- 2 ½ cups of water
- 1/2 pound of red or gold potatoes, diced
- 1 14 oz. of can diced tomatoes (or 1 1/2 cups diced fresh tomatoes), with their juices
- kosher salt and black pepper
- pinch of red pepper flakes, or to taste
- 1.5 to 2 pounds of boneless, skinless sea bass filets, cut into roughly 2″ pieces
- 2 tbsp. of fresh lemon juice (from about 1 lemon)
- 2 tbsp. of chopped fresh dill

Cooking Instructions:

1. Select the Sauté function on your Instant Pot to cook the onions in 2 tbsp. of olive oil, until browned and softened for about 3 minutes.

2. Add the garlic, and sauté until fragrant for about 30 seconds. Add the white wine to deglaze.

3. Scrap up any brown bits with a wooden spoon, until about half the wine has evaporated for about 1 minute.

4. Add the water, clam juice, potatoes, and tomatoes, plenty of salt and pepper, and red pepper flakes. Turn the "sauté" function off.

5. Close and lock the Lid in place, then select the Manual function, and cook on High Pressure for about 5 minutes.

6. When the time is up, do a quick pressure release until the float valve is depressed. Open your Instant Pot carefully and turn the Sauté function back on.

7. Once soup is simmering, add the fish pieces and simmer for 5 minutes, until fish is just cooked and flakes apart easily.

8. Turn off Sauté function, then stir in the lemon juice and fresh dill, along with the remaining 2 tbsp. of extra-virgin olive oil.

9. Taste and adjust seasoning if you desire.

10. Serve and enjoy.

Instant Pot Salmon

Preparation time: 10 minutes

Cooking time: 5 minutes

Total time: 15 minutes

Serves: 3 to 4

Ingredients:

- 3 medium lemon
- ¾ cup of water
- 4 fillet salmon
- 1 bunch of dill weed, fresh
- 1 tbsp. of butter, unsalted
- ¼ tsp. of salt
- ¼ tsp of black pepper, ground

Optional:

- 1 cup of brown rice, raw
- 4 cups of green beans

Cooking Instructions:

1. Add ¼ cup of fresh lemon juice, and ¾ cup of water in the bottom of your Instant Pot.

2. Add the steamer rack. Place the (Sockeye) salmon fillets, frozen, on top of the steamer rack.

3. Sprinkle fresh dill on top of the salmon, place one slice of fresh lemon on top of each one.

4. Close and lock the Lid in place, then select the Manual function, and cook on High Pressure for about 5 minutes.

5. When the time is up, select Cancel and do a quick pressure release.

6. Serve immediately with butter, extra dill and lemon, and salt and pepper.

7. Serve and enjoy!

Fish with Orange & Ginger Sauce

Preparation time: 10 minutes

Cook time: 7 minutes

Total time: 17 minutes

Serves: 4

Ingredients:

- 4 white fish fillets
- Juice and zest from 1 orange
- Thumb size piece of ginger, chopped
- 3 to 4 spring onions
- Olive oil
- Salt and pepper to taste
- 1 cup of fish stock or white wine

Cooking Instructions:

1. Dry the fish fillets with a paper towel.

2. Rub the olive oil on the fish fillets and season lightly.

3. Add the fish stock or white wine, spring onions, ginger, orange zest and juice into the bottom of your Instant Pot.

4. Place the fish into the steamer basket. Close and lock the lid in place.

5. Select Manual function to cook at high pressure for about 7 minutes.

6. Serve on top of an undressed garden salad and enjoy.

Fish Coconut Curry

Preparation time: 5 minutes

Cooking time: 3 minutes

Total time: 8 minutes

Serves: 4

Ingredients:

- 1 lb. tilapia filets, cut in 2-inch pieces
- 1 tbsp. of olive oil
- ½ tsp. of mustard seeds
- 1 can coconut milk
- 1 tbsp. of ginger-garlic paste OR ½ inch ginger + 3 cloves garlic, crushed or ground
- 10-15 curry leaves OR 2-3 kaffir lime leaves
- ½ medium onion, sliced
- ½ green pepper, sliced
- ½ orange or yellow pepper, sliced
- 1 tsp. of salt
- ½ tsp. of turmeric powder
- ½ tsp. of red chili powder
- 2 tsp. of coriander powder
- 1 tsp. of cumin powder
- ½ - 1 tsp. of garam masala
- 2-3 sprigs of cilantro
- 6-8 mint leaves, optional
- ½ tsp. of lime juice, added just before serving)

Cooking Instructions:

1. First, cut the tilapia in 2-inch pieces and slice the onions and bell peppers.

2. Chop the ginger-garlic for a few times in a mini-food processor. Press the Sauté setting and when it reads hot, add the oil and mustard seeds.

3. Once the mustard seeds start to splutter, add curry leaves and ginger-garlic paste and sauté for about 30 seconds.

4. Add the sliced onions and bell peppers and sauté for additional 30 seconds. Add together all the spices and give everything a good stir. Sauté for further 30 seconds.

5. Add the coconut milk and mix well. Bring the contents to a simmer for about 30 seconds to a minute to prevent the coconut milk from curdling under pressure.

6. Add the tilapia you have cut in to 2-inch pieces, a few cilantro sprigs and give everything a good stir to coat the fish with coconut milk.

7. You may add a few mint leaves on top to give the coconut curry a very mild and sweet minty aroma.

8. Close and lock the lid in place and ensure that the steam valve is in sealing position. Cook on Manual, high pressure for about 2-3 minutes.

9. When the time is up, use a quick pressure release. Finish the curry with a light squeeze of lime.

10. Serve with brown rice/white rice or a slice of toasted baguette and enjoy!

Mediterranean Style Fish

Preparation time: 5 minutes

Cook time: 12 minutes

Total time: 17 minutes

Ingredients:

- 4 white fish fillets, we used cod
- 1 pound (500g) of cherry tomatoes, halved
- 1 cup of black salt-cured olives OR Taggiesche, French or Kalamata
- 2 tablespoons of pickled capers
- 1 bunch of fresh thyme
- Olive oil
- 1 clove of garlic, pressed
- Salt and pepper to taste

Cooking Instructions:

1. Add about 1½ - 2 cups of water into the Instant Pot and trivet or steamer basket.

2. Line the bottom of the heat-proof bowl with cherry tomato halves to prevent the fish filet from sticking. Add the thyme and set a few springs aside for garnish.

3. Place the fish fillets over the cherry tomatoes, sprinkle with remaining tomatoes, crushed garlic, a dash of olive oil and a pinch of salt.

4. Insert the dish in the Instant Pot with a long aluminum sling. Set the pressure level to low and turn the heat up high.

5. Once the pan reaches pressure, reduce the heat and cook at high pressure for about 5 minutes.

6. When time is up, use a natural pressure release. Carefully open the lid and distribute the fish into individual plates, top with the cherry tomatoes.

7. Sprinkle with olives, capers, fresh thyme, a crackle of pepper and a little swirl of fresh olive oil.

8. Serve immediately and enjoy!

Instant Pot Shrimp

Ingredients:

- 2 pounds of shrimp
- 2 tablespoons of oil
- 2 tablespoons of butter
- 1 tablespoon of garlic, minced
- ½ cup of white wine
- ½ cup of chicken stock
- Pasta or cooked rice
- 1 tablespoon of lemon juice
- Parsley for garnish
- Salt & pepper to taste

Cooking Instructions:

1. Add the oil and butter in your Instant Pot and select the Sauté function.

2. When the butter is melted. Add in the garlic and cook until fragrant.

3. Then, add the white wine and chicken stock to deglaze the pot, and stir up any browned bits.

4. Turn off the Sauté function and add the shrimp. Then close and lock the Lid in place. Select the meat/stew function, set to cook for 1 minute.

5. When time is up, allow the Instant Pot to release pressure naturally for about 5 minutes.

6. Open the Lid and stir in the cooked pasta or rice and add the lemon juice, salt and pepper to taste. Use 2 cups of rice and 3 cups of water to cook rice in your Instant Pot.

7. Use the rice button on your Instant Pot and allow to release pressure naturally for about 10 minutes.

8. Use 2 cups of pasta to 3 cups of water to cook pasta in your Instant Pot. Use the soup button and cook for about 8 minutes, when time is up, do a quick pressure release.

9. Serve and enjoy!

Lemon Pepper Salmon

Preparation time: 5 minutes

Cooking time: 10 minutes

Total time: 15 minutes

Serves: 3 to 4

Ingredients:

- ¾ cup of water
- A few sprigs of parsley dill, tarragon, basil or a combo
- 1 lb. of salmon filet skin on
- 3 tsp. of ghee or other healthy fat divided
- ¼ tsp. of salt or to taste
- ½ tsp. of pepper or to taste
- ½ lemon thinly sliced
- 1 zucchini julienned
- 1 red bell pepper julienned
- 1 carrot julienned

Cooking Instructions:

1. Add water and herbs in your Instant Pot and then put in the Trivet, ensure that the handles are extended up.

2. Place salmon, skin down on rack. Then, drizzle salmon with ghee/fat, season with salt and pepper, and cover with lemon slices.

3. Close and lock the Lid in place and ensure that the valve is on sealing position.

4. Select the Steam function to cook for about 3 minutes. While salmon cooks, julienne your veggies.

5. When the time is up, do a quick pressure release. Select the Warm/Cancel button.

6. Remove lid carefully, then remove the rack with salmon and set on a plate. Remove the herbs and discard, add veggies. Then close and lock the Lid in place.

7. Select the Sauté function and allow the veggies cook for about 1 or 2 minutes.

8. Serve veggies with salmon and add remaining tsp. of fat to the pot and pour a little of the sauce over them if you like.

9. Serve and enjoy!

Drunken Clams

Preparation time: 10 minutes

Cooking time: 4 minutes

Total time: 14 minutes

Serves: 4 to 5

Ingredients:

- ¼ cup (60 ml) olive oil
- 2 cloves of garlic, peeled and minced
- ¼ cup of finely chopped fresh basil
- 2 cups of (500 ml) pale ale
- 1 cup of (250 ml) water
- ½ cup of (125 ml) chicken broth
- ¼ cup of (60 ml) dry white wine
- 3 pounds of (1.44 kg) fresh clams, scrabbled
- 2 tablespoons freshly squeezed lemon juice

Cooking Instructions:

1. Heat olive oil in your Pressure Cooker over medium heat.

2. Add minced garlic and cook, stirring, until fragrant, for 2 minutes. Then stir in chopped fresh basil.

3. Add in water, beer, chicken broth, wine and lemon juice. Increase heat to high and bring mixture to a boil.

4. Boil for about 1 minute, after boiling arrange a steamer rack and steamer basket in your Pressure Cooker. Place clams in basket, then close and lock the Lid in place.

5. Set the burner heat to High Pressure, when the pressure cooker reaches High Pressure, reduce the burner heat to low.

6. Set timer to cook for about 4 minutes. When the time is up, carefully open the Lid.

7. Discard any clams that have not opened. Transfer the cooked clams to a serving bowl using a tong. Pour cooking liquid over.

8. Serve and enjoy!

Instant Pot Mussels

Serves: 3 to 4

Ingredients:

- 2 tbsp. of butter
- 2 shallots, chopped
- 4 garlic cloves, minced
- ½ cup of broth
- ½ cup of white wine
- 2 pounds of mussels cleaned
- Lemon optional for serving
- Parsley optional for serving

Cooking Instructions:

1. Clean and remove beards from mussels.

2. Discard any mussels that do not close when tapped against a hard surface or have cracks.

3. Place the chopped onions and butter in your Instant Pot, select Sauté function. Stir and sauté onions until translucent.

4. Add garlic and cook for 1 minute before adding broth and wine. Then turn off the sauté setting and carefully add the mussels to your Instant Pot.

5. Select the Manual function, and cook on High Pressure for about 5 minutes.

6. When time is up. Allow the Instant pot to release pressure naturally.

7. Serve with a squeeze of lemon juice (if you like) and a sprinkle of parsley.

8. Serve and enjoy!

Poached Salmon

Serves: 4

Preparation time: 6 minutes

Cooking time: 4 minutes

Total time: 10 minutes

Ingredients:

- 16 oz. of salmon fillet with skin
- 4 scallions, trimmed
- Zest of 1 lemon
- 3 black peppercorns
- ½ tsp. of fennel seeds
- 1 tsp. of white wine vinegar
- 1 bay leaf
- ½ cup of dry white wine
- 2 cups of chicken broth
- ¼ cup of fresh dill
- Salt and Pepper

Cooking Instructions:

1. Place the basket into the bottom of your Instant Pot.

2. Season the fish with salt and pepper. Place the fillet in the basket.

3. Cover the fish with the broth, wine and vinegar and add the remaining ingredients.

4. Close and lock the lid in place and ensure that the valve is in sealing position.

5. Lower the heat to medium low and cook at high pressure for about 4 minutes.

6. When the time is up, use a natural pressure release. Carefully open the lid and remove the salmon and place on serving plate.

7. Pour the remaining broth over the fish.

8. Serve and enjoy.

Pasta with Tuna and Capers

Preparation time: 2 minutes

Cook time: 10 minutes

Total time: 12 minutes

Ingredients:

- 1 tbsp. of olive oil
- 1 garlic clove
- 3 anchovies
- 2 cups of tomato puree
- 1½ tsp. of salt
- 16 ounces (500g) fusilli pasta
- 2 5.5 ounces (160g) cans Tuna packed in olive oil
- Enough water to cover
- 2 tbsp. of capers

Cooking Instructions:

1. Press the Sauté function and add the oil, garlic and anchovies.

2. Sauté' the contents until the anchovies start to break up and the garlic cloves are just starting to turn golden.

3. Add together the tomato puree and salt and mix together.

4. Pour in the un-cooked pasta and the 1 tuna can (5 ounces) mixing to coat the dry pasta evenly.

5. Flatten the pasta in an even layer and pour enough water to cover.

6. Close and lock the lid in place and ensure that the steam valve is in sealing position.

7. Cook for about 3 minutes at low pressure. When time is up, use a natural pressure release.

8. Carefully remove the lid and mix in the remaining 5 ounces of tuna and sprinkle with capers.

9. Serve immediately and enjoy.

New England Fish Chowder

Ingredients:

- 2 tablespoons of butter or oil
- 1 large onion, finely chopped
- 3 stalks celery, finely chopped
- 1 large carrot, finely chopped
- 1 lb. of potatoes, peeled and cut into 1/2-inch, diced.
- 1 lb. of thick firm white fish, such as cod, cut into 1 1/2-inch chunks
- 2 cups fish stock or clam juice
- 1 cup cold water
- 1 bay leaf
- ½ teaspoon of dried thyme
- 1 – 1 ½ cups of milk, half & half, or heavy cream
- 1 cup of fresh or frozen (defrosted) corn kernels
- ¼ cup of finely chopped fresh parsley

Cooking Instructions:

1. Press the Sauté function and add the butter to melt.
2. Generously season the freshly ground white or black pepper to taste.
3. Add the onion and sauté until soften for about 2-3 minutes.
4. Add in the celery, carrot, and potatoes and sauté for further 1 minute.
5. Add the fish chunks, stock, water, bay leaf, and thyme.
6. Close and lock the lid in place and ensure that the steam valve is in sealing position.
7. Cook at high pressure for about 4 minutes. When the time is up, do a quick-release method.
8. Carefully open the lid and remove the bay leaf and stir in the milk, corn, parsley, and salt and pepper to taste.
9. Simmer the contents until the corn is cooked and the chowder is hot.
10. Transfer to a serving plate and top with additional butter if needed.
11. Serve immediately and enjoy.

Salmon and Veggies

Ingredients:

- 1 frozen 5-7 oz. of salmon filet
- Chopped and sliced veggies such as carrots, celery, cabbage, onion and broccoli
- Mc cormick cedar plank salmon seasoning, (Costco) or use your desired seasonings
- ¼ cup of dry sherry, you may substitute with ¼ cup of water and ½ tsp. of chicken better than bullion
- Salt and pepper to taste

Cooking Instructions:

1. Chop and slice your desired veggies.

2. Add the chopped veggies to a 7x3" round cake pan.

3. Season with salt and pepper to taste and add the dry sherry.

4. Lightly cover the pan with foil. Add 1 cup of water into the bottom of your Instant Pot.

5. Place the trivet with the pan on top, then lay a second trivet on it with the salmon on top.

6. Close and lock the lid in place and ensure that the steam valve is in sealing position.

7. Select Manual and set to cook at high pressure for about 5 minutes. When the time is up, use a quick pressure release.

8. Serve and enjoy.

Salmon Biryani

Ingredients:

- 10 ounces of salmon fillet
- 3 cloves of diced garlic
- Juice of 1/2 lime
- A pinch of salt and pepper
- 1 tbsp. of finely chopped mint leaves
- 1 tbsp. of turmeric powder
- 1 tbsp. of red chili flakes
- 1-inch piece of grated ginger
- ½ tbsp. of cumin
- ½ tbsp. of crushed coriander seeds
- ½ tbsp. of crushed cardamom seeds
- ½ tsp. of cinnamon powder
- ¼ tsp. of cloves
- ¼ tsp. of nutmeg grated
- 1 medium sized onion diced
- 2 cups of basmati rice
- 3 cups of stock or water
- Fresh chopped cilantro for garnish, optional

Cooking Instructions:

1. In a medium bowl, add together all of the ingredients and marinate for about 1 hour.

2. Rinse the basmati rice under cold water and remove as much starch as possible.

3. Add the rice into the bottom of your Instant Pot and add the marinated salmon along with all of the remaining marinate on top of the rice.

4. Add the 3 cups of stock or water. Close and lock the lid in place and ensure that the steam valve is in sealing position.

5. Set it to manual, high pressure for about 5 minutes. When the time is up, use a quick pressure release.

6. Carefully open the lid and give everything a good stir.

7. Garnish with chopped cilantro.

8. Serve and enjoy!

Shrimp Paella

Preparation time: 10 minutes

Cooking time: 5 minutes

Total time: 15 minutes

Serves: 3 to 4

Ingredients:

- 1 pound of jumbo shrimp, shell and tail on frozen
- 1 cup of Jasmine rice
- 4 tablespoons of butter
- 1 onion chopped
- 4 cloves of garlic chopped
- 1 red pepper chopped
- 1 cup of chicken broth
- ½ cup of white wine
- 1 teaspoon of paprika
- 1 teaspoon of turmeric
- ½ teaspoon of salt
- ¼ teaspoon of black pepper
- 1 pinch of saffron threads
- ¼ teaspoon of red pepper flakes
- ¼ cup of cilantro optional

Cooking Instructions:

1. Select the Sauté function on your Instant Pot. Then add butter to your Instant Pot and melt.

2. Add onions and cook until softened. After cooking onions add garlic and cook for about 1 minute more.

3. Add in paprika, turmeric, salt, black pepper, red pepper flakes, and saffron threads to your Instant pot. Stir well and cook for 1 minute.

4. Add red peppers, rice and stir thoroughly. Then, cook for about 30 seconds to 1 minute.

5. Add in chicken broth and white wine, ensure that all rice is covered. Add shrimp on top.

6. Turn off your Instant Pot. Close and lock the Lid in place, ensure that the valve is on sealing position.

7. Select the Manual function, and cook on High Pressure for about 5 minutes.

8. When the time is up, do a quick pressure release. Remove shrimp from pot and peel if desired.

9. Serve with cilantro and enjoy!

Spicy Pineapple Shrimp

Preparation time: 10 minutes

Cooking time 2: minutes

Total time: 12 minutes

Serves: 3 to 4

Ingredients:

- 1 large red bell pepper, cleaned and sliced
- 12 oz. Calrose cice or quinoa
- ¾ cup of unsweetened pineapple juice
- ¼ cup of dry white wine
- 2 tbsp. of soy sauce
- 2 tbsp. of Thai sweet chili sauce
- 1 tbsp. of sambal oelek ground chili paste
- 1 lb. of Large Shrimp, tails on frozen
- 4 Scallions chopped, white and greens separated
- 1.5 cups of unsweetened pineapple chunks drained

Cooking Instructions:

1. Drain Juice from Pineapple and reserve Pineapple Chunks aside.

2. Measure out ¾ cup of Pineapple Juice, then add Red Bell Peppers, Pineapple Juice, Wine, Chili Sauce, Soy Sauce, Sambal Oelek, Rice and chopped Scallions (the white part) to your Pressure Cooker.

3. Place frozen Shrimp on top, then secure the Lid ensuring that the valve is on sealing position.

4. Select Manual function, and cook on High Pressure for 2 minutes.

5. When the time is up, allow the Pressure cooker to release pressure naturally for about 10 minutes.

6. Add Pineapple Chunks and Scallion Greens and mix thoroughly.

7. Serve and enjoy!

Savory Shrimp with Tomatoes and Feta

Preparation time: 10 minutes

Cooking time: 12 minutes

Total time: 22 minutes

Serves: 5 to 6

Ingredients:

Cook Together:

- 2 tbsp. of Butter
- 1 tbsp. of garlic
- ½ tsp. of red pepper flakes adjust to taste
- 1.5 cups of chopped onion
- 1 14.5 ounces of can tomatoes
- 1 tsp. of oregano
- 1 tsp. of salt
- 1 lb. of frozen shrimp 21 to 25 count, shelled

Add After Cooking

- 1 cup of crumbled feta cheese
- ½ cup of sliced black olives
- ¼ cup of parsley

Cooking Instructions:

1. Select the Sauté function on your Instant Pot.

2. Once it is hot, add the butter. Allow it to melt a little, then add garlic and red pepper flakes.

3. Add in onions, tomatoes, oregano and salt. Then, pour in the frozen shrimp.

4. Set the Instant pot to LOW pressure 1 minute. When the time is up, do a quick pressure release.

5. Mix in the shrimp with the rest of the lovely tomato broth. Allow it to cool slightly. Right before serving.

6. Sprinkle the feta cheese, olives, and parsley if you desire.

7. Serve immediately and enjoy.

Creamy Chipotle Shrimp Soup

Preparation time: 5 minutes

Cooking time: 25 minutes

Total time: 30 minutes

Serves: 4 to 5

Ingredients:

- 3 slices bacon, chopped
- 1 cup of onion, diced
- ¾ cup of celery, chopped
- 1 teaspoon of garlic
- 1 tablespoon of flour
- ¼ cup of dry white wine
- 1 ½ cups of chicken or vegetable broth
- ½ cup of whole milk
- 1 ½ cups of potatoes, cut into small (1/3-inch) cubes
- 1 cup of frozen corn kernels
- 2 teaspoons of diced canned chipotle peppers in adobo sauce
- ¾ teaspoon of salt
- ½ teaspoon ground black pepper
- ½ teaspoon of dried thyme
- ½ pound of shrimp, peeled and deveined
- ¼ cup of heavy cream

Cooking Instructions:

1. Set your Instant Pot to Sauté function.

2. Add bacon to inner pot of Instant Pot and Sauté until crisp, for about 3 minutes, stirring frequently.

3. Then, add in onions, celery and garlic. Sauté till vegetables have softened, for about 2 to 3 minutes.

4. Stir in flour and allow to cook for 30 seconds to 1 minute, Select Cancel function and add white wine to deglaze the pot.

5. Stir to remove brown bits from the bottom of your Pot. If not completely deglazed, add 1 or 2 tablespoons of broth.

6. Stir in broth, milk, potatoes, corn, Chipotle, salt, black pepper and thyme.

7. Secure the lid and select the Manual function, and cook on High Pressure for 1 minute.

8. When the time is up, do a quick pressure release. Stir in shrimp and cream.

9. Close and lock the Lid in place, Allow the shrimp to cook in the residual heat for 10 minutes.

10. Garnish each serving with scallions, parsley and/or crumbled bacon.

11. Serve and enjoy!

Shrimp Risotto

Preparation time: 5 minutes

Cook time: 10 minutes

Total time: 15 minutes

Servings: 6

Ingredients:

- 1 cup of jasmine rice
- 1 cup of water
- 2 tbsp. of butter
- 1 tbsp. of lemon juice
- ¼ cup of frozen vegetables
- 1 lb. of frozen raw shrimp
- ¼ cup of shredded Parmesan cheese
- A pinch of salt
- Pepper, to taste

Cooking Instructions:

1. Press the Sauté function and add the butter to melt.

2. Add the rice, water, lemon juice, salt and pepper to taste. Place the frozen shrimp and frozen vegetables on top.

3. Lay the veggies on top half submerged in the water.

4. Cook at High Pressure for about 5 minutes. When the time is up, use a quick pressure release.

5. Give everything a good mix. Allow the water to absorb back into rice if desired.

6. Serve with Parmesan cheese and enjoy.

Oyster Stew

Preparation time: 5 minutes

Cook time: 6 minutes

Total time: 11 minutes

Serves: 4

Ingredients:

- 1-pint of organic heavy cream OR full fat coconut milk for dairy free
- 1 cup of bone broth
- 1 cup of minced celery
- 2 10 ounces of jars shucked oysters with liqueur
- 2 tablespoons of grass-fed butter OR coconut oil for dairy free
- 2 tablespoons of minced shallot
- 2 cloves garlic minced
- ½ teaspoon of sea salt
- ¼ teaspoon of white pepper
- 2 tablespoons of fresh parsley, chopped

Cooking Instructions:

1. Press the Sauté function and add the butter to melt.

2. Add the shallot, garlic and celery until soft for about 4 minutes. Add the oysters, cream and broth.

3. Close and lock lid in place. Select Manual to cook at low pressure for about 6 minutes.

4. When the time is up, use a quick pressure release. Stir in the sea salt and white pepper to taste.

5. Snip the oysters using kitchen shears, if needed.

6. Ladle into serving plates and garnish with parsley.

7. Serve and enjoy.

CHAPTER 6: BEEF

Homemade Hamburger

Preparation time: 6 minutes

Cooking time: 4 minutes

Total time 10 minutes

Serves: 5 to 6

Ingredients:

- 1 lb. of ground beef
- 2 cups of beef broth
- 16 ounces of cheddar cheese
- 4 ounces of American cheese
- 1 tablespoon of onion powder
- 1 tablespoon of garlic powder
- 16 ounces of elbow macaroni
- 8 ounces of milk or heavy cream

Cooking Instructions:

1. Sauté ground beef and seasonings until crumbled and meat changes pink color.

2. Pour in uncooked pasta and broth. Secure the lid in place and ensure that the valve is in sealing position.

3. Select the Manual function, and cook on High Pressure for about 4 minutes.

4. Do a quick pressure release, add milk and Stir in both kinds of cheese slowly.

5. Serve and enjoy!

Cheesesteak Sloppy

Preparation time: 10 minutes

Cooking time: 10 minutes

Total time: 20 minutes

Serves: 5 to 6

Ingredients:

- 1 ½ pounds of ground beef
- 1 tablespoon of butter
- 1 chopped green bell pepper
- 2 tablespoons of ketchup
- 1 tablespoon of Worcestershire sauce
- ¼ cup of water
- 1 package Lipton Onion Soup Mix
- 8 ounces of provolone chopped
- Hamburger buns or sub rolls.

Cooking Instructions:

1. Select the Sauté function on your Instant Pot.

2. Add butter, bell pepper and ground beef. Cook until the ground beef changes its pink color.

3. Add ketchup, Worcestershire sauce, water, and Lipton onion soup mix.

4. Select the Manual function, and cook on High Pressure for about 6 minutes.

5. When the timer beeps, add in cheese and mix until melted.

6. Serve with your favorite cheesesteak toppings on a hamburger.

7. Serve and enjoy!

Beef and Macaroni

Preparation time: 10 minutes

Cooking time: 5 minutes

Total time: 15 minutes

Serves: 5 to 6

Ingredients:

- 1 lb. of ground beef (or turkey (or turkey, chicken, Italian sausage, rabbit, bison)
- 1 lb. of cavatappi or other macaroni
- 1 tbsp. of extra virgin olive oil
- ½ onion diced well
- ½ green bell pepper diced (optional)
- 3 cloves fresh garlic minced fine
- 28 oz. of pureed tomatoes
- 15 oz. of tomato sauce
- 3 oz. of tomato paste
- 1 tbsp. of Worcestershire sauce (2 tbsp. if using turkey)
- 2 tsp. of dried basil
- 2 tsp. dried parsley flakes
- 2 tsp. of sea salt
- 1 tsp. of light brown sugar
- ¼ tsp. of crushed red pepper flakes
- ¼ tsp. of freshly ground black pepper
- ¼ cup of dry red wine a good Cabernet!
- 2.5 cups fresh water

Cooking Instructions:

1. Select the Sauté function on your Pressure Cooker and allow it to heat.

2. Then add in olive oil to your Pressure Cooker cooking pot. Dump in the beef and break into pieces as you brown.

3. When meat is partially brown, add in onions (and peppers, if using) and sauté until meat is mostly brown.

4. Add in garlic and Sauté for 1 minute more, drain excess grease, if needed.

5. Add the rest of the ingredients. Secure the lid and ensure that the valve is on sealing position.

6. Select the Manual function, and cook on High pressure for about 5 minutes.

7. When the time is up, allow a 5 minutes natural pressure release, then do a quick pressure release. Top with freshly grated cheese.

8. Serve and enjoy!

Instant Pot Spaghetti

Preparation time: 10 minutes

Cooking time: 10 minutes

Total time: 20 minutes

Serves: 5 to 6

Ingredients:

- 1 pound of ground beef or leave out if you wish
- ¼ cup onion diced
- 1 teaspoon of garlic minced
- 1 jar spaghetti sauce (24 oz)
- 2 cups of water
- 8 ounces spaghetti noodles
- 2 tablespoons of olive oil
- 1 teaspoon of salt optional, to taste

Cooking Instructions:

1. Select the Sauté function on your Instant Pot.

2. Add in olive oil, onions, and garlic and cook until onions are softened a bit.

3. Add in ground beef and cook until the ground beef changes its pink color. Drain grease or leave in, your choice.

4. Set your Instant Pot to Manual, High Pressure. Then add jar of spaghetti sauce, water, break noodles into thirds and push noodles into liquid until they are covered. Remember Don't stir.

5. Close and lock the Lid, ensure that the valve is on sealing position.

6. Set to cook for 10 minutes. When the time is up, do a quick pressure release.

7. Then stir and serve.

Meatball Subs

For Meatballs:

- 2 pounds of ground beef
- ½ white onion, diced
- ½ cup of bread crumbs
- 2 eggs
- 1 tbsp. of minced garlic
- 1 bunch of cilantro, optional
- 1 tsp. of salt
- 1 tsp. of pepper

For Sauce:

- 1 large can tomato sauce
- 1 small can diced fire roasted tomatoes
- ½ white onion diced
- 6 chopped leaves of fresh basil

Cooking Instructions:

1. In a medium bowl, mix together the bread crumbs, eggs, meat, onion, garlic and spices.

2. Use your hands to mix the ingredients to combine. Roll small amounts of the mixture into balls and set inside the instant pot.

3. When you're done making all the meatballs, pour the tomato sauce, the fire roasted tomatoes and diced onion into the bottom of your Instant Pot.

4. Chop the basil and sprinkle it on top of all the ingredients. Select Manual and cook at high pressure for about 15 minutes.

5. When the time is up, use a natural pressure release.

6. Carefully open the lid when it has depressurized.

7. Serve on organic hoagie buns and enjoy!

Stuffed Pepper Casserole

Preparation time: 10 minutes

Cooking time: 10 minutes

Total time: 20 minutes

Serves: 7 to 8

Ingredients:

- 2 bell peppers, diced
- 1 pound of ground beef
- ½ onion diced
- 1 can chilies diced, 4 ounces
- 2 cups of HemisFares spaghetti sauce
- 1 cup of diced tomatoes I prefer petite version, canned
- 1 ½ cups of white rice uncooked
- 2 cups of water or vegetable broth
- ½ teaspoon of chili powder or more
- 1 teaspoon seasoned salt or more, to taste
- 1 cup of mozzarella or parmesan cheese shredded
- 1 tablespoon of olive oil
- ½ teaspoon of minced garlic

Cooking Instructions:

1. Add olive oil to your Instant pot. Select the Sauté function on your Instant Pot, normal or low and start to brown your ground beef.

2. When it is still slightly pink add in diced bell peppers and onion. Then continue to cook together until onions and peppers are soften and beef is browned.

3. Turn off your Instant Pot. Leave the ground beef on the bottom of your pot and pour in spaghetti sauce.

4. Add the diced tomatoes, spices, chilies, uncooked rice, and either water or vegetable broth on top. Remember don't stir

5. Secure the lid and ensure that the valve is on sealing position. Select the Manual function, and cook on Low Pressure for about 10 minutes.

6. When the time is up, do a quick pressure release and stir.

7. Serve topped with mozzarella cheese and enjoy.

Barbacoa Beef

Yield: 9

Servings: 4

Ingredients:

- 5 cloves garlic
- ½ medium onion
- 1 lime, juice
- 2-4 tablespoon of chipotle's in adobo sauce
- 1 tablespoon of ground cumin
- 1 tablespoon of ground oregano
- ½ teaspoon of ground cloves
- 1 cup of water
- 3 pounds of beef eye of round or bottom round roast, all fat trimmed
- 2 ½ tsp. of kosher salt
- Black pepper to taste
- 1 teaspoon of oil
- 3 bay leaves

Cooking Instructions:

1. Add the garlic, onion, lime juice, cumin, oregano, chipotles, cloves and water in a blender and puree until smooth.

2. Trim off the fat from the meat, cut into 3-inch pieces. Generously season with 2 tsp. of salt and black pepper to taste.

3. Press the Sauté function, add the oil and brown the meat in batches on all side for about 5 minutes. Add the sauce from the blender and bay leaves.

4. Select Manual function to cook at high pressure for about 65 minutes or until the meat is tender. When the time is up, remove the meat and place in a dish.

5. Use two forks to shred the meat, reserve the liquid and discard the bay leaf. Add the shredded meat back to the Instant Pot.

6. Add ½ tsp. of salt or to taste, ½ teaspoon of cumin and 1 ½ cups of the reserved liquid.

7. Serve and enjoy!

Beef and Potato Au Gratin

Preparation time: 5 minutes

Cook time: 25 minutes

Total time: 30 minutes

Servings: 5-6

Ingredients:

- 1 pound of browned ground beef, well-seasoned with salt and pepper
- 4-5 large uncooked russet potatoes, peeled and sliced in 1/4" slices
- 1 ½ cup of shredded cheddar or sharp cheese
- ¾ cup of chicken broth
- 1 tablespoon of Italian seasoning, we used a blend of basil, marjoram, oregano and thyme.
- 1 teaspoon of paprika
- ½ teaspoon of salt
- ¼ teaspoon of pepper
- 2 teaspoon of olive oil

Cooking Instructions:

1. Add the olive oil in the bottom of your Instant Pot and use a napkin to swipe it evenly around to coat evenly.

2. In a medium bowl, combine together the Italian seasoning, paprika, salt, and pepper.

3. Layer the sliced potatoes, then sprinkle a portion of the ground beef, and top with shredded cheese in your Instant Pot.

4. Season to taste with 1/3 of the seasoning you place in the bowl. Layer the potatoes, ground beef, cheese, and additional seasoning.

5. Pour about ¾ cup of chicken broth. Close and lock the lid in place and seal the valve.

6. Select Manual function to cook at high pressure for about 15 minutes. When the time is up, use a natural pressure release and dish into bowls.

7. Serve and enjoy!

Beefy Broccoli Rice

Ingredients:

- 1.5 pounds of ground beef
- 3.5 cups of water
- 1.5 cups of white rice
- 12 ounces of frozen chopped broccoli
- 1 jar double cheddar pasta sauce
- 1 teaspoon of onion powder
- 1 teaspoon of garlic powder

Cooking Instructions:

1. Add the ground beef into the bottom of your Instant Pot.

2. Select the Sauté function and brown the ground beef. Once the beef has browned, add in the rice and water.

3. Ensure that the rice flattens enough to be covered with water. Close and lock the lid in place.

4. Select Manual function to cook on high pressure for about 7 minutes. When the time is up, do a quick pressure release.

5. Add the pasta sauce, onion powder and garlic powder, followed by the broccoli. Press the Steam setting to cook for about 3 minutes.

6. When the time is up, give everything a good stir.

7. Serve and enjoy!

Vegetable Beef Soup

Ingredients:

- 2 pounds of lean ground beef
- 1 large onion, diced
- 2 teaspoons of garlic, minced
- 1 can (14.5 oz) stewed tomatoes, with liquid
- 3 cups of beef broth
- 4 carrots, sliced into round disks
- 3 stalks of celery, sliced or diced
- 3 to 4 medium-large potatoes, cut into bite-sized chunks
- 3 tablespoon of tomato paste
- ½ teaspoon of salt
- ½ teaspoon of pepper
- 2 teaspoon of dried parsley flakes
- ½ teaspoon of ground oregano

Cooking Instructions:

1. Select the Sauté function on your Instant Pot.

2. Then add ground beef, onion, and garlic and sauté until beef is cooked through.

3. Drain off as much of the oil as you can. After draining add can of stewed tomatoes with liquid, breaking up the tomatoes into small pieces.

4. Stir in beef broth, diced vegetables, tomato paste, and seasonings. Secure the Lid and ensure that the valve is on sealing position.

5. Select the Manual function, and cook for about 4 minutes. When the time is up, do a quick pressure release. remove the lid.

6. Serve and enjoy!

Sweet Potato Chili

Preparation time: 5 minutes

Cooking time: 20 minutes

Total time: 25 minutes

Ingredients:

- 1 tsp. of olive oil
- 1 medium onion, diced
- 3 garlic cloves minced
- ½ lb. of ground pork
- 1 lb. of ground beef
- 1 large sweet potato peeled and cut into 1/2-inch pieces
- 3 celery stalks sliced
- 3 ½ cups or 1 (28-ounce) can crushed tomatoes
- 1 tbsp. of Worcestershire sauce or coconut aminos
- 1 tsp. of cumin
- 1 tsp. of chili powder
- salt and pepper to taste

Optional toppings:

- Diced avocado

Cooking Instructions:

1. Select the Sauté function on your Instant.

2. Add in olive oil and diced onion to the interior pot. Sauté until tender and then add minced garlic, ground pork, and ground beef.

3. Cook, stirring frequently, until the pork and beef are browned. Add in sweet potato, celery, crushed tomatoes, Worcestershire sauce, cumin, and chili powder.

4. Give everything a good stir to combine well and situate the top onto the Instant Pot. Select the Manual function, and cook on High Pressure for about 10 minutes.

5. When the time is up, Allow the Instant Pot to release pressure naturally and then carefully release the rest pressure before removing the Lid.

6. Serve the chili with any additional toppings desired.

7. Serve and enjoy!

Instant Pot Goulash

Preparation time: 10 minutes

Cooking time: 4 minutes

Total time: 14 minutes

Serves: 5 to 6

Ingredients:

- 1 pound of ground beef
- 1 large onion
- 3 cloves of garlic
- 2 15- oz. cans tomato sauce
- 2 15- oz. cans diced tomatoes
- 2 tablespoons of Italian seasoning
- 3 tablespoons of soy sauce
- 3 cups of elbow noodles
- 2 ½ cups of water
- 3 bay leaves
- salt and pepper to taste

Cooking Instructions:

1. Select the Sauté function on your Instant Pot.

2. Once it is hot, add ground beef garlic, salt, pepper, and onion. Then cook until the meat changes color to brown.

3. Drain fat then add tomato sauce, diced tomatoes, Italian seasoning, soy sauce, water, noodles, and bay leaves.

4. Select the Manual function, and cook on High Pressure for about 4 minutes.

5. When the time is up, do a quick pressure release. Take out the bay leaves and give everything a good stir.

6. Top with Parmesan Cheese and enjoy.

Beef Stroganoff

Ingredients:

- 2 tbsp. of olive oil
- ¾ pound of ground beef or turkey
- ½ cup of chopped red onion
- 1 tbsp. of garlic
- 4 oz. sliced Mushroom
- 2 10.5 oz. cans Campbell's condensed French onion soup
- 2 cups of water
- Salt to taste
- Pepper to taste
- 1 tbsp. of cornstarch)
- ¾ bag of egg noodles
- ½ cup of Greek yogurt or sour cream

Cooking Instructions:

1. Spray Instant Pot interior with cooking spray.

2. Select the Sauté function on your Instant Pot to sauté. Drizzle 1 tbsp. cooking oil.

3. Add the brown ground beef or turkey, onion, and garlic. Drain excess grease and return to pot.

4. Add mushrooms and sauté for another 1 or 2 minutes. Add water, onion soup, salt, pepper and mix well.

5. Whisk in cornstarch, add noodles. Secure the lid in place. Select the Manual function, and cook on High Pressure for about 6 minutes.

6. When the time is up, allow the pressure to release naturally for about 5 minutes, and then do a quick pressure release.

7. Stir in Greek Yogurt until combined.

8. Serve and enjoy!

Instant Pot Bolognese

Preparation time: 15 minutes

Cooking time: 45 minutes

Total time: 60 minutes

Ingredients:

- 4 oz. of pancetta (or center cut bacon), chopped
- 1 tbsp. of unsalted butter
- 1 large white onion, minced
- 2 celery stalks (about 3/4 cup), minced
- 2 carrots (about 3/4 cup), minced
- 2 pounds of lean ground beef
- ¼ cup of dry white wine, such as Pinot Grigio
- 2 (28 ounces) cans crushed tomatoes (I love Tuttorosso)
- 3 bay leaves
- ½ tsp. of kosher salt and fresh black pepper, to taste
- ½ cup half & half cream
- ¼ cup chopped fresh parsley

Cooking Instructions:

1. Select the Sauté function on your Instant Pot, Sauté the pancetta over low heat until the fat melts, for about 4 to 5 minutes.

2. Add in the butter, onion, celery and carrots and cook until soft, for about 6 to 7 minutes. Add the meat and season it with ¾ tsp. of salt and black pepper to taste.

3. Sauté until browned, for about 4 to 5 minutes, breaking the meat up into smaller sizes with a wooden spoon as it cooks.

4. Pour in the wine and cook until it reduces down, for about 3 to 4 minutes. Add crushed tomatoes, bay leaves, ¾ tsp. of salt and fresh cracked black pepper.

5. Secure the Lid, select the Manual function, and cook on High Pressure for about 15 minutes.

6. When the time is up, allow the pressure to release naturally, stir in the half & half and garnish with parsley.

7. Serve over your favorite pasta, zucchini noodles or spaghetti squash. Enjoy.

Instant Pot Picadillo

Preparation time: 5 minutes

Cooking time: 15 minutes

Total time: 20 minutes

Serves: 4 to 5

Ingredients:

- 1 to 1 ½ pounds of lean ground beef
- 1 medium chopped onion
- 4 to 5 cloves garlic, minced
- 1 red bell pepper, finely chopped or, 1 pound of sweet mini peppers, diced
- 4 tbsp. of cilantro
- 1 tomato, finely chopped
- 1 teaspoon of ground cumin
- ½ teaspoon of paprika
- ½ teaspoon of garam marsala
- 1 teaspoon of salt
- ¼ teaspoon of black pepper
- 2 bay leaves
- 3 tbsp. of green olives or capers, finely chopped + juice
- 3 ounces tomato sauce
- 2 ounces of water

Cooking Instructions:

1. Select the Sauté function on your Instant Pot, combine the meat and season with pepper, salt, garam masala, paprika, chili powder and cumin.

2. Make use of your spoon to break up the meat into small sizes and sauté until the meat changes pink color.

3. Add in the onion, garlic, pepper, ½ of the cilantro, and tomato and sauté in with the beef approximately 2 to 3 minutes.

4. Add in the bay leaf, tomato sauce and water and mix well. Secure the Lid, ensure that the valve is on sealing position.

5. Select the Manual function, and cook on High Pressure for about 5 minutes. When the time is up, do a quick pressure release. Stir in the remaining cilantro.

6. Serve over rice and enjoy!

Mongolian Beef

Preparation time: 3 minutes

Cooking time: 17 minutes

Total time: 20 minutes

Serves: 3 to 4

Ingredients:

- 1 ½ pounds of Flank steak
- ¾ cup of soy sauce
- ½ cup of brown sugar
- ¼ cup of water
- ½ tsp. of fresh ginger minced
- 1 garlic clove minced
- 1 carrot shredded
- 1 tbsp. of olive oil
- 1 green onion sliced (garnish)

To thicken Sauce:

- 3 tbsp. of cornstarch
- 3 tbsp. of water

Cooking Instructions:

1. In a medium bowl, slice flank steak into strips, combine soy sauce, water, oil, sugar, ginger, and garlic.

2. Add sauce in the instant pot, then add beef strips and shredded carrot. Mix until the beef is coated in the sauce.

3. Select the Manual function, and cook on High Pressure for about 8 minutes. When the time is up, allow the pressure to release naturally for about 10 minutes.

4. Combine the water and the cornstarch in a medium bowl until there are no lumps. Select the Sauté function on your Instant Pot.

5. Pour in the cornstarch mixture. Allow the sauce to boil until it thickens for about 1 to 2 minutes. Pour the beef into a platter and garnish with green onions.

6. Serve and enjoy!

Cheeseburger Macaroni

Preparation time: 15 minutes

Cook time: 3 minutes

Total time: 19 minutes

Servings: 5

Calories: 553 kcal

Ingredients:

- 1 cup of elbow macaroni uncooked
- 1 cup of water
- 1 pound of ground beef or turkey
- 3 tablespoon of olive oil
- 1/3 onion, diced
- 1 teaspoon of salt, optional
- 1 teaspoon of garlic powder
- 1 can cheddar cheese soup
- ½ - 1 cup of sour cream
- 1 cup of cheddar cheese shredded

Cooking Instructions:

1. Pres the Sauté function and add the olive oil and ground beef.

2. Brown the beef, add the diced onions and cook together until the ground beef is no longer pink.

3. Press Cancel to stop the Sauté function. Drain the grease and return pot. In a medium bowl, whisk together the water and cheddar cheese soup. Pour the mixture on top of the ground beef.

4. Pour the uncooked noodles in and avoid stirring, gently push down the noodles to submerge in the liquid.

5. Close and lock the lid in place. Select Manual function to cook at high pressure for about 3 minutes. When the time is up, use a natural pressure release.

6. Set the Instant Pot to sauté mode and add the sour cream and shredded cheese. Slowly stir and let it to come to a boil and bubble.

7. It will thicken for about 1 to 2 minutes. Serve topped with more cheese and enjoy!

CHAPTER 7: PORK

Ground Pork Casserole

Preparation time: 10 minutes

Cooking time: 20 minutes

Total time: 30 minutes

Serves: 5 to 6

Ingredients:

- 1 pound of ground pork
- 2 cups of diced raw potatoes
- 1 ½ cups of sliced carrots
- 1 cup of chopped celery
- ½ cup of chopped onion
- 1 cup of frozen peas
- 1 cup of frozen whole kernel corn
- 1 10 ounces can tomato soup
- ½ cup of water
- 1 teaspoon of dried parsley flakes
- salt and pepper to taste

Cooking Instructions:

1. Select the brown function on your Instant Pot, brown meat, onion, and celery. (If your device doesn't have a browning setting, you can use large skillet).

2. Combine meat mixture, potatoes, carrots, peas, and corn. Stir in tomato soup, water, parsley flakes, salt, and pepper, and give everything a good stir.

3. Secure the Lid and select the Manual function, to cook on High Pressure for about 20 minutes.

4. When the time is up, do a quick pressure release.

5. Serve and enjoy!

Pork Chops with Gravy

Preparation time: 5 minutes

Cooking time: 20 minutes

Total time: 25 minutes

Serves: 3 to 4

Ingredients:

- 5 pork chops bone in or out
- 1 tbsp. of olive oil
- 1 tsp. of salt
- ½ tsp. of garlic powder
- ½ tsp. of pepper
- 1 envelope ranch dressing mix
- 1 one oz. envelope brown gravy mix
- 1 10.5 oz. can cream of chicken soup
- 2 cups of beef broth
- 2 tbsp. of cornstarch
- 2 tbsp. of water

Cooking Instructions:

1. Season the pork chops on both sides with the salt, garlic powder, and pepper.

2. Select the Sauté function on your Instant Pot and add in olive oil.

3. Once the oil is hot brown the pork chops on each side for 2 to 3 minutes just until browned.

4. Remove the pork chops from your Instant Pot, pour in ¼ cup of the beef broth to your Instant Pot and use a wooden spoon to deglaze the bottom of the pot.

5. Turn off your Instant Pot, add the pork chops along with the ranch dressing mix, brown gravy mix, cream of chicken soup, and remaining beef broth to the pot.

6. Secure the Lid and ensure that the valve is on sealing position. Select Manual function, and cook for about 8 minutes.

7. When the time is up, allow to release pressure naturally for about 10 minutes. After natural pressure release, release the remaining pressure.

8. Carefully remove the lid. Transfer the pork chops from the pot to a serving plate. Whisk together the cornstarch and water in a medium bowl.

9. Select the Sauté function on your Instant Pot and whisk in the cornstarch mixture. Whisk constantly until gravy is thick, then, turn off your instant pot.

10. Serve the pork chops with the gravy and your favorite side dishes.

11. Serve and enjoy!

Pulled Pork

Preparation time: 35 minutes

Cooking time: 45 minutes

Total time: 1 hour 5 minutes

Serves: 8 to 9

Ingredients:

- 4 pounds of boneless pork loin or boneless pork shoulder/butt
- 1 teaspoon of kosher salt
- ½ teaspoon of black pepper
- 1 to 2 chipotle peppers in adobo sauce, minced
- 12 ounces Dr pepper soda
- your favorite BBQ sauce

Cooking Instructions:

1. Slice pork into 4 pieces and season with salt and pepper.

2. Place pork in your instant pot, insert and top with minced chipotle peppers.

3. Pour Dr pepper around the pork. Then secure the Lid and ensure that the valve is on sealing position.

4. Select the Manual function, and cook for about 45 minutes. When the time is up, allow to release pressure naturally for about 15 minutes.

5. After natural pressure release, do a quick pressure release to get rid of the remaining pressure.

6. Transfer the pork to a large mixing bowl (it will be so tender it may start to fall apart during the transfer).

7. Shred the pork with two forks and add BBQ sauce to your tastes.

8. Serve and enjoy!

Pork Lettuce Wraps

Preparation time: 15 minutes

Cook time: 1 hour 15 minutes

Total time: 1 hour 30 minutes

Servings: 4

Calories: 544 kcal

Ingredients:

- 1 cup of dried wheat berries
- 1 tablespoon of peanut oil
- 1 lb. of ground pork lean
- 8 scallions, thinly sliced
- ¼ cup of cilantro leaves, minced
- ¼ cup of lime juice fresh
- 2 tablespoon of fish sauce
- 2 tablespoons of light brown sugar
- 1 teaspoon of sambal oelek
- 2 heads of boston lettuce

Cooking Instructions:

1. Pour the wheat berries into the bottom of your Instant Pot.

2. Pour 3 cups of water. Close and lock the lid into place and ensure that the steam valve is in sealed position.

3. When the time is up, use a natural pressure release for about 10 minutes. Carefully open the lid and drain the wheat berries in a colander.

4. Press the Sauté setting and heat the oil. Add the ground pork and cook until it has cooked through for about 5 minutes, crumbling with a wooden spoon.

5. Add the scallions, cilantro, lime juice, fish sauce, brown sugar and sambal oelek.

6. Turn off the Instant Pot and add the wheat berries.

7. Scoop about 2 tbsp. into each lettuce leaf.

8. Serve immediately and enjoy.

Pork Carnitas

Ingredients:

- 2 ½ lb. of trimmed, boneless pork shoulder blade roast, cut into 4 pieces
- 2 tsp. of kosher salt
- Black pepper, to taste
- 6 cloves garlic, cut into sliver
- 1 ½ tsp. of cumin
- ½ tsp. of sazon, we used homemade
- ¼ tsp. of dry oregano
- 1 cup of reduced sodium chicken broth
- 2-3 chipotle peppers in adobo sauce
- 2 bay leaves
- ¼ tsp. of dry adobo seasoning
- ½ tsp. of garlic powder

Cooking Instructions:

1. Generously season the pork with salt and pepper.

2. Press the Sauté button and add the oil to brown the pork on all sides for about 5 minutes.

3. Remove from the heat and let to cool. Using a sharp knife, insert blade into pork about 1-inch deep and insert the garlic slivers.

4. Generously season the pork with cumin, sazon, oregano, adobo and garlic powder on each side.

5. Pour the chicken broth, add the chipotle peppers and give everything a good stir. Add the bay leaves and put the pork back into the Instant Pot.

6. Close and lock the lid in place. Select Manual to cook at high pressure for about 80 minutes.

7. When the time is up, open the lid and shred the pork using two forks.

8. Combine with the juices that are at the bottom. Remove the bay leaves and adjust cumin and add adobo to your desired taste.

9. Serve and enjoy!

Sloppy Joes

Ingredients:

- 1 pound of ground beef
- ½ medium onion, chopped
- 4 garlic cloves minced
- ½ cup of beef broth
- ½ cup of ketchup
- 2/3 cup of chopped green bell pepper
- ½ cup of celery, chopped
- 2/3 tbsp. of brown sugar
- 1 tbsp. of tomato paste
- 2 tbsp. of prepared mustard
- 1 tbsp. of cider vinegar
- 2 tbsp. of Worcestershire sauce
- ½ tbsp. of chili powder
- ¼ cup of water
- 1 tbsp. of corn starch

Cooking Instructions:

1. Press the Sauté button on your Instant Pot.

2. In a medium bowl, mix together the ketchup, brown sugar, tomato paste, mustard, vinegar, chili powder, and Worcestershire then set aside.

3. When the pot reads hot, add in hamburger and garlic. Cook until the meat begins to brown then drain fat.

4. Add the meat back into the bottom of your Instant Pot. Add celery, peppers, and onion. Cook the contents for about 1 to 2 minutes until fragrant.

5. Turn off the Instant Pot and add the ketchup mixture and beef broth. Select Manual to cook on high pressure for about 7 minutes.

6. When the time is up, use a quick pressure release. In a medium bowl, mix together the water and corn starch.

7. Turn the Instant Pot back onto sauté setting and add the corn starch mixture. Cook for about 1 to 2 minutes until the sauce thickens. Give everything a good stir.

8. Serve on buns and enjoy.

Pork Chili

Preparation time: 10 minutes

Cooking time: 30 minutes

Total time: 40 minutes

Serves: 6 to 7

Ingredients:

- 2 tbsp. of olive oil
- ½ sweet onion, chopped
- 3 garlic cloves, minced
- 1 red bell pepper, diced {seeds removed}
- 2 tbsp. of tomato paste
- 1 tsp. of salt
- 1 lb. of ground pork
- 3 tbsp. of chili powder
- 2 tsp. of cumin
- 1 tsp. of paprika
- ¼ tsp. of coriander
- 1 tsp. of Mexican oregano {or regular oregano}
- 1 – 16 oz. can of black beans, drained and rinsed
- 1 – 16 oz. can of corn, drained and rinsed
- 1 – 16 oz. can of fire roasted diced tomatoes {or regular diced tomatoes}
- 2 – 6 oz. cans of diced chiles
- 2 cups of stock {you can use vegetable, chicken or beef}

Garnish:

- Sour cream
- Cheese
- Cilantro
- Red Onion
- Jalapeno

Cooking Instructions:

1. Select the Sauté function on your Instant Pot and add in 2 tbsp. of olive oil.

2. Add the onion, bell peppers and garlic and sauté until tender, for about 3 to 4 minutes.

3. Add the tomato paste and sauté for 1 minute more. Then add 1 tsp. of salt and the pork and continue to sauté until the pork is almost cooked through.

4. Add the spices and Sauté until the pork is cooked through and the spices are aromatic.

5. Add in all of the remaining ingredients and give everything a good stir to combine.

6. Secure the Lid, select Manual function, and cook on High Pressure for about 15 minutes.

7. When the time is up, do a quick pressure release.

8. Adjust seasonings to your tastes and garnish with your favorite toppings

9. Serve immediately and enjoy!

Pork Green Chili

Serves: 7 to 8

Ingredients:

- 3 lb. of pork shoulder, trimmed of excess fat and cut into 1-inch cubes
- Kosher salt and freshly ground black pepper
- 3 tbsp. of vegetable oil
- 2 lb. of tomatillos, peeled and quartered
- 3 poblano peppers, seeded and diced
- 3 jalapeno peppers, seeded and diced
- 1 yellow onion, diced
- 4 cloves of garlic, minced
- 1 tbsp. of ground cumin
- 4 cups of chicken broth
- 1 bunch fresh cilantro, chopped
- Tortilla chips, for serving
- Shredded Mexican cheese blend, for serving
- Diced red onion, for serving
- Diced avocado, for serving

Cooking Instructions:

1. Select the Sauté function on your Instant Pot. While the pot is heating, season pork with salt and black pepper.

2. Once the bottom of the pot is hot, then add the oil and cook the pork shoulder in batches until browned on all sides, for about 5 to 10 minutes.

3. Transfer the pork to a plate. Repeat with remaining pork until all pork is browned.

4. Return pork to the pot and add in tomatillos, peppers, onion, garlic, cumin and chicken broth.

5. Secure the Lid, and select the Manual function, to cook for 30 minutes.

6. When the time is up, do a quick pressure release and open the lid carefully.

7. Stir in cilantro and season to taste with salt and pepper. Serve with tortilla chips, cheese, red onion, and avocado.

8. Serve and enjoy!

Spicy Pork & Spinach Stew

Preparation time: 10 minutes

Cooking time: 30 minutes

Total time: 40 minutes

Serves: 3 to 4

Ingredients:

- 1 large onion
- 4 cloves garlic
- 10 oz. of Rotel
- 1 tsp. of dried thyme
- 2 tsp. of tony chachere seasoning or other cajun seasoning blend
- 1 lb. of pork butt or beef meat cut into 2-inch chunks

For Finishing:

- ½ cup of heavy whipping cream
- 4 to 6 cups of chopped baby spinach

Cooking Instructions:

1. Blend onion, garlic, and Rotel together.

2. If you don't have Rotel, use 14 ounces can of tomatoes and 5 ounces can of green chilis (poblano-style).

3. Pour into your Instant Pot, then add the Tony chachere or other Cajun seasoning mix.

4. Add in the pork/beef cubes and give everything a good stir. Secure the Lid and ensure that the valve is on sealing position.

5. Select the Meat function, and cook for about 20 minutes. When the time is up, allow it to release pressure naturally for about 10 minutes and then get rid of the remaining pressure.

6. Select the Sauté function on your Instant Pot. When the stew starts to boil, add the cream and give everything a good stir. Add the spinach leaves and cook until wilted.

7. Serve and enjoy!

Pork Stew with Fall Vegetables

Preparation time: 15 minutes

Total time: 50 minutes

Total time: 1 hour 5 minutes

Serves: 3 to 4

Ingredients:

- 1 ½ pounds of pork shoulder cubes
- 3 tbsp. of olive oil
- 1 onion, chopped
- 1 red bell pepper, seeded and diced
- 2 cloves garlic, chopped
- 1 rutabaga, peeled and cubed
- 4 carrots, peeled and cut into large pieces
- 8 whole baby potatoes
- 1 can diced tomatoes
- ½ cup of chicken broth
- Salt and pepper

Cooking Instructions:

1. In a large skillet over high heat, brown the pork in 2 tablespoons (30 ml) of the oil. season with salt and pepper. And reserve aside.

2. In a Pressure Cooker over medium heat, soften the onion, bell pepper and garlic in the remaining oil (1 tablespoon/15 ml).

3. Add in the pork, rutabaga, potatoes, carrots, tomatoes and broth. season with salt and pepper.

4. Secure the Lid, cook on High Pressure for about 20 minutes.

5. When the time is up, allow it to release pressure naturally.

6. Serve immediately and enjoy!

Pork and Hominy Stew

Preparation time: 10 minutes

Cooking time: 50 minutes

Total time: 1 hour

Ingredients:

- 1 ¼ lb. od boneless pork shoulder, trimmed of fat and cut into 4-inch pieces
- Kosher salt and fresh cracked pepper
- 1 tablespoon of olive oil, divided
- 1 medium white onion, chopped
- 4 garlic cloves, minced
- 2 tbsp. of chili powder
- 4 cups of low sodium chicken broth
- 2 cups of water
- 2 (15 oz) cans hominy, drained and rinsed
- 4 ounces diced avocado and lime wedges, for serving
- cilantro for garnish

Cooking Instructions:

1. Season the pork with salt, then select the Sauté function and heat half of the oil.

2. Add in the pork and cook until pieces are browned on all sides, for about 8 minutes. Remove it from your pot and transfer to a plate.

3. Add the remaining oil, onion, garlic, and chili powder and sauté until soft, for about 4 minutes.

4. Add the broth and water, then cook. Stir and scrap up the brown bits with a wooden spoon. Return pork to your Pressure Cooker. Close and lock the Lid in place.

5. Cook on high pressure until meat is tender, for about 45 minutes. When the time is up, do a quick pressure release.

6. Then, remove lid carefully. Skim fat if any, use two forks to shred the pork.

7. Stir in hominy and heat through. Serve with avocado and lime and garnish with cilantro.

8. Serve and enjoy!

Coca-Cola Pulled Pork

Preparation time: 15 minutes

Cooking time: 1 hour 30 minutes

Total Time 1 hour 45 minutes

Serves: 7 to 8

Ingredients:

- 2 tablespoons of olive oil
- 4 pounds of boneless pork shoulder
- 1 teaspoon of salt
- 1 teaspoon of pepper
- 1 teaspoon of garlic powder
- 1 teaspoon of onion powder
- 1 teaspoon of smoked paprika
- ¼ cup of brown sugar
- 16 oz. Coca-Cola
- 3 cloves garlic
- 1 ½ cups of BBQ sauce, divided

Cooking Instructions:

1. Select the Sauté function on your Instant Pot Set. Add in oil to Instant Pot and allow oil to get hot.

2. Use tongs to sear all sides of your pork shoulder. If it doesn't fit in one piece you can cut it into 4 smaller pieces.

3. In a small bowl, mix all dry spices and brown sugar. Sprinkle over all sides of the pork shoulder. Place pork shoulder in the Instant Pot.

4. Pour Coca-Cola in your Instant Pot. Add garlic cloves. Add half of the BBQ sauce in Instant Pot. (If you want more liquid you can add ¼ cup of chicken or vegetable broth).

5. Secure the Lid, select the Meat/Stew function, and cook for about 90 minutes. When the time is up, allow it to release pressure naturally.

6. Remove pork shoulder and place it on a cutting board. Pull the meat apart with two forks.

7. Select the Sauté function on your Instant Pot. Heat up sauce left inside and add the remaining half of your BBQ sauce.

8. Heat thoroughly. Add 1 teaspoon of corn starch to sauce if you would like a thicker sauce.

9. Add meat back into Your Instant Pot. Stir until sauce coats the meat perfectly.

10. You can leave in Instant Pot on keep warm or remove and place in a bowl.

11. Serve and enjoy!

CHAPTER 8: BEANS, RICE & GRAINS

Tomatillo Poblano White Beans

Preparation time: 5 minutes

Cook time: 35 minutes

Total time: 40 minutes

Servings: 6

Ingredients:

- 2 cups of chopped tomatillos
- 1 cup of chopped poblano, seed and stems removed before chopping
- 1 cup of chopped onion
- ½ Jalapeño, without seeds
- 1 ½ teaspoon of ground cumin
- 1 ½ cups of dried great northern beans, soaked for about 8 to 12 hours and drained
- 1 ½ cups of water
- 2 teaspoons of dried oregano
- Salt and Pepper to taste

Cooking Instructions:

1. Place the tomatillos, poblano, onion and jalapeño into the blender or food processor.

2. Pulse the veggies until they are tiny pieces, but not pureed. Press the sauté setting over medium heat and pour in the blended veggies.

3. Add the cumin and give everything a good stir to combine. Cook for about 4 minutes or until the edges of the onions are removed and the cumin more fragrant.

4. Add the beans, water and oregano to the sauté mixture and give everything a good stir to combine. Close and lock the lid in place and ensure that the steam valve is in sealing position.

5. Cook on Manual setting at High Pressure to cook for about 35 minutes. When the time is up, use a natural pressure release.

6. If there is still more liquid in the pot, return the pot back to the sauté setting and simmer to allow some of the liquid to evaporate. Add salt and pepper to taste to suit your desired taste.

7. Serve and enjoy.

Red Beans and Rice

Servings: 10

Calories: 563 kcal

Ingredients:

- 1 medium onion diced
- 1 bell pepper diced
- 3 celery stalks diced
- 3 cloves garlic minced
- 1 lb. of dry red kidney beans
- 1 teaspoon of salt
- ½ teaspoon of black pepper
- ¼ teaspoon of white pepper, optional
- 1 teaspoon of hot sauce, we used Texas Pete
- 1 teaspoon of fresh thyme or ½ teaspoon of dried thyme
- 2 leaves bay
- 7 cups of water
- 1 lb. of chicken andouille sausage cut into thin slices
- 10 cups of cooked rice

Cooking Instructions:

1. Place all of the ingredients to the Instant Pot except for sausage and rice.

2. Close and lock the lid in place. Select Manual High Pressure to cook for about 28 minutes.

3. When the time is up, use a quick pressure release.

4. Carefully open the lid and add the chicken andouille sausage.

5. Close and lock the lid in place. Select Manual setting to cook at High Pressure for about 15 minutes.

6. Carefully open the lid and allow the beans mixture to sit for some minutes to thicken the liquid.

7. Serve the bean mixture over a cup of cooked rice and enjoy.

Chicken and Brown Rice

Serves: 8

Ingredients:

- 1 medium onion
- 3 clove garlic
- 2 cups of carrots, baby
- 2 cups of mushrooms, brown, Italian
- 2 cups of brown rice, raw
- 1 tbsp. of olive oil
- 2 ¼ cup of chicken broth, low-sodium
- 2 lbs. of chicken thigh, boneless, skinless
- 1/8 tsp. of salt
- 1/8 tsp. of black pepper, ground
- 1 can (10.75 ounces) soup, cream of chicken, canned, condensed
- 2 tbsp. of Worcestershire sauce
- 1 tbsp. of thyme, fresh

Cooking Instructions:

1. Press the "Sauté" setting. While the Instant Pot is heating, dice the onion, mince garlic, and chop veggies.

2. Rinse and drain the rice. Once the pot reads "Hot," add the oil and sauté the onions for about 3 minutes.

3. Push "Cancel" to stop the sauté function. Mix the veggies, garlic, rice, and broth into the pot.

4. Place the chicken on top, add salt and pepper, then cover with cream of chicken soup and Worcestershire sauce. Add about 8-10 small sprigs of thyme on top.

5. Close and lock the lid in place and ensure that the steam valve is in sealing position.

6. Select "Manual" function and set the brown rice to cook at high pressure for about 25 minutes and white rice for about 20 minutes.

7. When the time is up, use a quick pressure release for about 2 minutes. Carefully open the lid and remove the thyme sprigs.

8. Stir the pot to shred chicken and mix in any extra liquid.

9. Serve hot and enjoy.

Rice Pudding

Preparation time: 5 minutes

Cook time: 14 minutes

Total time: 19 minutes

Servings: 5

Calories: 198 kcal

Ingredients:

- 1 cup of uncooked rice
- ½ cup of sugar
- 1 cup of water
- 1.5 tablespoon of butter
- 2 cups of milk 2% or whole is best
- 1 egg
- ¼ cup of evaporated milk
- ½ teaspoon of vanilla
- ½ teaspoon of almond extract, optional
- A pinch of nutmeg, optional
- A pinch of cinnamon, optional

Cooking Instructions:

1. Press the Sauté setting and add the butter until melted.

2. Add the rice and stir so rice is coated. Add the milk, water, vanilla, cinnamon, almond extract if using and sugar. Give everything a good stir to combine.

3. Close and lock the lid in place and close steam valve. Select Manual, High Pressure to cook for about 14 minutes. When the time is up, carefully open the lid.

4. In a medium bowl, whisk together the egg and evaporated milk. Spoon a spoonful of rice pudding mixture into egg mixture and stir to combine.

5. Add additional warm spoonful of rice mixture and give everything a good stir. Add the bowl full of egg mixture into the bottom of your Instant Pot and press the sauté function.

6. Let to be hot enough and bubble for about 30-60 seconds, stir slowly when it starts to bubble so it doesn't stick to bottom. It will start to thicken.

7. Serve hot or chilled, top with cinnamon or nutmeg and enjoy.

Perfect Rice

Preparation time: 5 minutes

Cook time: 8 minutes

Total time: 13 minutes

Ingredients:

- 1 cup of rice
- 1 cup of water
- 1 teaspoon of cooking oil
- 1 pinch of salt

Cooking Instructions:

1. Rinse the rice under cold running water until the water.

2. Add the oil into the bottom of your Instant Pot together with the rinsed rice, water and salt.

3. Close and lock the lid in place and ensure that the steam valve is set to the "sealing" position.

4. Press the "Rice" function. When the time is up, use a natural pressure release for about 10 minutes.

5. Carefully open the lid and fluff the rice with a fork.

6. Serve and enjoy.

Chickpea Curry with Brown Rice

Preparation time: 10 minutes

Cook time: 20 minutes

Total time: 30 minutes

Ingredients:

For Chickpea Curry:

- 1 tbsp. of vegetable oil
- 1 medium red onion, chopped
- 2 tbsp. of Chana masala
- 1 tbsp. of garlic, minced
- 1 tbsp. of fresh ginger, minced
- 1 cup (250ml) dried chickpeas, soaked overnight or quick-soaked
- 1 cup (250ml) water
- 1 can 14.5 ounces (400g) chopped tomatoes
- 1 tsp. of sea salt

For Bain Marie Brown Rice:

- 1½ cups (375ml) of brown rice
- 2 cups (500g) of water

Cooking Instructions:

1. Add the rice and water in a 4-cup capacity heat proof container.

2. Press the Sauté function and add the oil. Add the onion and sauté' until it is just starting to caramelize for about 7 minutes.

3. Add the Chana masala powder, garlic, and ginger and sauté' for additional 30 seconds until the garlic starts to cook.

4. Pour in the water, chickpeas and tomato. Lower the steamer basket into the chickpea curry and add the uncovered heat-proof container onto the steamer basket.

5. Close and lock the lid in place and ensure that the steam valve is in sealing position.

6. Cook for about 20 minutes at high pressure. When the time is up, use a natural pressure release for about 10 minutes.

7. Carefully open the lid and remove the heat-proof container. Fluff the rice and place on a serving plate.

8. Mix-in the salt in the curry in the base of the Instant Pot and spoon it out.

9. Serve with a sprinkling of raw red onion slices and a dollop of low-fat yogurt.

10. Serve and enjoy.

Black Bean & Lentil Chili

Preparation time: 5 minutes

Cook time: 30 minutes

Total time: 35 minutes

Ingredients:

- 1 tbsp. of olive oil
- 1 medium red onion, chopped
- 2 medium carrots, chopped
- 1 tbsp. of paprika
- 1 tbsp. of dried oregano
- 2 tsp. of garlic powder
- 2 tsp. of powdered cumin
- 1 oz. (30g) dried mushrooms, we used Porcini
- 1 cup (200g) lentils, sorted and rinsed
- 2 cups (400g) dry black beans, soaked overnight and rinsed
- 1 - 14 ounces can (400g) chopped tomatoes OR 1¾ cups of freshly chopped tomatoes
- 4 cups of water
- 2 tbsp. of Worcestershire sauce
- 1 tsp. of salt
- grated cheddar cheese, optional
- quick-pickled jalapeño peppers, optional

Cooking Instructions:

1. Press the "Sauté'" setting and chop the carrots and onion.

2. Add the oil and add the onion to sauté. Add the paprika, oregano, garlic powder and cumin, dried mushrooms, carrots, and chopped tomatoes.

3. Give everything a good mix. Mix-in the lentils, black beans and water.

4. Close and lock the lid in place and set the valve to the sealing position. Cook for about 10 minutes at high pressure.

5. When the time is up, use a natural pressure release. Carefully open the lid add salt and Worcestershire sauce. Give everything a good mix.

6. Garnish with grated cheddar cheese and quick-pickled jalapeño peppers if desired

7. Serve and enjoy.

Steamed Brown Rice

Preparation time: 1 minute

Cook time: 30 minutes

Total time: 31 minutes

Ingredients:

- 2½ cups (625ml) of water
- 2 cups (500ml) of brown rice

Cooking Instructions:

1. Add all of the ingredients into the bottom of your Instant Pot.
2. Give everything a good stir.
3. Close and lock the lid in place and ensure that the steam valve is set in sealing position.
4. Cook for about 20 minutes at high pressure.
5. When the time is up, use a natural pressure release for about 10 minutes.
6. Carefully remove the lid and give everything a good stir.
7. Fluff with a fork and serve immediately.

Santa Fe Beans and Rice

Preparation time: 10 minutes

Cook time: 20 minutes

Total time: 30 minutes

Servings: 6

Ingredients:

For the Beans and Rice:

- 1 ½ cups of long grain brown rice
- 1 ¾ cups of water
- 1 (15 ounces) of can kidney beans, rinsed and drained
- 1 (15 ounces) of can black beans, rinsed and drained
- 1 (15 ounces) of can corn, rinsed and drained
- 1 (8 ounces) of can tomato sauce
- ½ cup of picante sauce, we used mild
- 2 tablespoons of taco seasoning
- 1 teaspoon of salt
- ½ teaspoon of pepper
- 1 ½ pounds of boneless, skinless chicken thighs or breasts, optional
- Grated cheddar, for serving

For the Garlic Lime Sour Cream:

- 1 cup of sour cream
- ¼ cup of chopped cilantro
- 1 teaspoon of lime zest
- 2 teaspoons of lime juice
- ½ teaspoon of kosher salt
- 2 garlic cloves, minced

Cooking Instructions:

1. Into the bottom of your Instant Pot, add the rice, water, kidney beans, black beans, corn, tomato sauce, picante sauce, taco seasoning, salt and pepper to taste.

2. Give everything a good stir. Close and lock the lid in place and ensure that the steam valve is set in sealing position.

3. Select Manual and set to cook at high pressure for about 20 minutes.

4. When the time is up, use a natural pressure release for about 10 minutes.

5. Carefully open the lid and give everything a good stir.

6. Prepare the garlic lime sour cream by stirring together sour cream, cilantro, lime zest, lime juice, kosher salt and garlic cloves.

7. Serve the rice and beans with a dollop of the sour cream on top.

8. Sprinkle with grated cheddar, if needed.

9. You can store the leftovers in an airtight container in the refrigerator for up to a week.

CHAPTER 9: VEGAN & VEGETARIAN

Spiced Potato Spinach Lentils

Preparation time: 10 minutes

Cook time: 30 minutes

Total time: 40 mins

Servings: 3

Calories: 200 kcal

Ingredients:

- 1/3 cup of uncooked brown lentils
- 1 teaspoon of oil
- 4 cloves of garlic, minced
- 1-inch ginger, minced
- 1 hot green chili, chopped
- 2 large tomatoes chopped
- ½ teaspoon of garam masala
- ¼ teaspoon of cinnamon
- ¼ teaspoon of cardamom
- ½ teaspoon of turmeric
- 2 medium potatoes cubed
- ¾ teaspoon of salt
- 1 cup of water
- 5 to 6 ounces of spinach

Cooking Instructions:

1. Add the lentils in a bowl and soak for about 1 hour.

2. Press the Sauté function over medium and add the oil, ginger, garlic, chili and cook until translucent.

3. Add the tomato, spices and cook until the tomatoes are tender.

4. Mash the larger pieces for about 4-5 minutes. Add the potatoes, drained lentils, spinach, water, salt and give everything a good stir.

5. Close and lock the lid in place and ensure that the steam valve is in sealing position.

6. Select Manual function to cook at High Pressure for about 7 to 8 minutes.

7. When the time is up, use a natural pressure release. Carefully remove the lid, taste and adjust the salt and spice to taste.

8. Add more spices or garam masala if desired. Garnish with cilantro, pepper flakes and lemon.

9. Serve over rice or with roti/flatbread and enjoy.

Quinoa with Miso, Mushrooms & Peppers

Preparation time: 15 minutes

Cook time: 15 minutes

Total time: 30 minutes

Serves: 4

Ingredients:

- 1 + ½ cups of uncooked quinoa
- 3 tbsp. of olive oil
- 1 brown onion, finely diced
- 10 medium button mushrooms, diced
- ½ long red chili, finely diced
- Pinch of salt
- 2 medium bell peppers (red and green), sliced or diced
- 2 cloves of garlic, grated or finely diced
- 2 tbsp. of raw brown miso paste
- 1 tbsp. of tomato paste
- 2 tbsp. of soy sauce or Tamari sauce
- 2 tbsp. of lemon juice
- 1 + ¼ cups of vegetable stock
- Fresh cilantro or parsley

Cooking Instructions:

1. Soak the quinoa in cold water and ½ tsp. of salt for about 15 to 20 minutes.

2. Rinse the soaked quinoa and strain through a sieve and set aside. Press the Sauté function and add the olive oil.

3. Add the chopped onions, mushrooms, chill and salt.

4. Give everything a good stir and cook for about 4-5 minutes, until softened.

5. Add the quinoa and the remaining ingredients and stir through.

6. Press the Keep Warm/Cancel function to cancel the sautéing function.

7. Close and lock the lid in place. Select to Manual, High Pressure to cook for 7 minutes.

8. When the time is up, use a natural pressure release for about 5 minutes. Use quick release to release any remaining pressure.

9. Carefully remove the lid and give everything a good stir. Taste and adjust the seasoning with salt and pepper to taste.

10. Serve with a side of vegetables or a salad and enjoy.

Beet Risotto with Thyme & Goat's Cheese

Preparation time: 20 minutes

Cook time: 15 minutes

Total time: 35 minutes

Serves: 4

Ingredients:

- 1 medium brown onion, finely diced
- 1 tbsp. of butter
- 1 tsp. of sea salt
- 1+1/2 cups of Arborio risotto rice
- 300 g / 0.5 pounds of beets, 1 large or 2 small beets, peeled and diced into small cubes
- 3 cloves of garlic, finely diced
- Zest of ½ lemon
- 3-4 sprigs of fresh thyme, leaves only, or 1 tsp. of dried thyme leaves
- 3 + ½ cups vegetable stock

For Finishing:

- Juice of ½ lemon
- 40 g / 1.5 ounces of Parmesan cheese, finely grated, about ½ cup
- ½ tbsp. of butter
- Pinch of ground black pepper

For Serving:

- 60 g / 2 ounces of soft goat's cheese such as chèvre, broken into small pieces
- A few extra sprigs of thyme

Cooking Instructions:

1. Press the Sauté function and add the onions, butter and salt.

2. Cook the contents for about 3 to 4 minutes, stirring a few times, until softened.

3. Add the rice, diced beets, garlic, lemon zest and thyme leaves and give everything a good stir.

4. Add the vegetable stock and stir through and ensure that you scrape down any rice kernels from the walls of the Instant Pot.

5. Close and lock the lid in place and ensure that the steam valve is set to sealing position.

6. Press the Manual function key and set to High Pressure and adjust the timing for 5 minutes.

7. When the time is up, use a natural pressure release for about 5 minutes before using quick release to release any remaining pressure.

8. Carefully remove the lid and stir in the Parmesan cheese, a little extra butter, lemon juice, and pepper.

9. Serve with crumbled goat's cheese and extra sprigs of thyme on top if desired.

Carrot Lemongrass & Cilantro Soup

Preparation time: 5 minutes

Cook time: 15 minutes

Total time: 20 minutes

Serves: 4

Ingredients:

- ½ large brown onion, roughly sliced
- 2 lemongrass sticks, cut in halves
- 3 large carrots, sliced in thick pieces
- 1 large sweet potato, peeled and roughly cut
- 1 large celery stick, roughly cut in 3-4 pieces
- Handful of fresh cilantro, both leaves and stems
- 2 large cloves of garlic
- 1 can of coconut milk
- 2 cups vegetable or chicken stock
- ½ red or green chili, diced roughly
- 2 tbsp. of soy sauce or fish sauce
- 1 tsp. of sea salt
- Juice of ½ lime
- Fresh cilantro and sesame seeds, for garnish

Cooking Instructions:

1. Add all of the ingredients into the bottom of your Instant Pot except for lime juice and stir through.

2. Close and lock the lid in place and ensure that the steam valve is set to sealing position.

3. Press the Manual function and set to High pressure for about 7 mins. When the time is up, use a natural pressure release for about 5-10 minutes.

4. Carefully open the lid and remove the lemongrass piece. Pour the soup's content to a blender or a food processor in 2-3 batches.

5. Puree the soup until smooth and transfer to another saucepan. Add the lime juice, stir through and add more salt or fish sauce to taste.

6. Serve with sesame seeds and fresh cilantro over the top and enjoy.

Barbacoa Mushroom Tacos

Preparation time: 10 minutes

Cook time: 30 minutes

Total time: 40 minutes

Servings: 3

Calories: 176 kcal

Ingredients:

- 2 large guajillo chilies
- 1 teaspoon of oil
- 1 bay leaf
- 1 large onion, thinly sliced or chopped
- 7 cloves of garlic, finely chopped
- 2 chipotle chilies in adobo sauce, 1 for less heat
- 1 teaspoon of ground cumin
- ½ teaspoon of dried oregano
- ½ teaspoon of smoked hot paprika or 1 teaspoon of chili powder blend
- ¼ teaspoon of ground cinnamon ¼ teaspoon of ground cloves
- ¼ teaspoon of salt
- ¾ cup of water or veggie broth
- 1 teaspoon of apple cider vinegar
- 1 to 3 teaspoon of lime juice
- ¼ teaspoon of sugar or maple, optional
- 8 ounces of sliced or chopped mushrooms white, cremini

Toppings:

- Avocado salsa or onions, lime juice, pepper and salt to taste

Cooking Instructions:

1. Place the guajillo chilies to soak in hot water for about 15 mins.

2. Heat the oil in a skillet over medium heat and add the bay leaf, onions, garlic and salt to taste.

3. Cook the contents until translucent for about 5 minutes and transfer half of the onion mixture to a blender.

4. Add the mushrooms to the rest of the onion mixture in the skillet and keep on cooking over medium heat.

5. Remove the stem and seed box from the soaking guajillo chili and place the chili to the blender.

6. Add the remaining sauce ingredients to the blend except the vinegar and lime.

7. Blend the ingredients until smooth and add all the blended sauce in the skillet.

8. Cover and cook in your pressure cooker for about 25-30 minutes or until mushrooms are tender.

9. Give everything a good stir and add additional water if the sauce is too thickened. Add in the vinegar and lime and cook for further 3-5 minutes.

10. Taste and adjust the seasoning with salt and flavor. Remove the bay leaf.

11. Serve over warm tortillas with avocado and chopped onion and baby greens of choice.

12. You can also add a dash of lime, freshly ground black pepper and salt to taste.

13. Serve and enjoy.

Vegan Lasagna Soup

Preparation time: 10 minutes

Cook time: 20 minutes

Total time: 30 minutes

Servings: 3

Calories: 327 kcal

Ingredients:

- 1 teaspoon of oil
- ½ onion, chopped
- 4 cloves of garlic, chopped
- 1 cup of veggies such as a combination of peppers, carrots, zucchini
- ¼ cup of red lentils, uncooked
- 1 cup of tomato puree
- 1-1.5 cup of diced tomato
- 2 teaspoons of Italian seasoning OR 1 teaspoon of basil, ½ teaspoon of oregano, parsley, a dash of thyme/sage and rosemary
- ¼ teaspoon each of onion powder, garlic powder
- ½ - ¾ teaspoon of salt
- 2 cups of water or veggie broth
- 5 ounces of lasagna sheets, broken into small pieces, or your favorite pasta
- A pinch of black and white pepper
- Pepper flakes, to taste
- 1 tablespoon of nutritional yeast
- 1 cup packed spinach, optional
- Vegan pesto, vegan ricotta or mozzarella, vegan butter/ garlic bread to serve, optional

Cooking Instructions:

1. Press the Sauté function key and heat the oil.

2. Once hot, add the onion, garlic and a pinch of salt to taste.

3. Cook the content for about 2 minutes, stirring occasionally.

4. Add your veggies and mix in. Add the red lentils, tomato, salt, seasoning, onion powder, garlic powder and give everything a good mix.

5. Add 1 tablespoon of tomato paste for additional tomato flavor if desired. Add the lasagna sheets and water and mix in.

6. Close and lock the lid in place and ensure that the steam valve is set in sealing position.

7. Select Manual function and set to cook at High Pressure for about 3 minutes.

8. When the time is up, use a natural pressure release for about 10 minutes.

9. Carefully remove the lid and mix in the black pepper, pepper flakes and nutritional yeast.

10. Taste and adjust the taste with salt and flavor. Add additional salt, broth, and lemon if desired.

11. Fold in the spinach if using and allow to sit for about 2 minutes.

12. Serve with pesto/basil and/or vegan ricotta/mozzarella, and garlic bread and enjoy.

Chickpea Spinach Curry

Preparation time: 10 minutes

Cook time: 40 minutes

Total time: 50 minutes

Servings: 4

Calories: 209 kcal

- **Ingredients:**
- ¾ cup of dried chickpeas soaked in warm water for about 4 hours
- 1 teaspoon of oil
- ½ medium onion, finely chopped
- 1 hot green chili, finely chopped
- 4-5 cloves of garlic, minced
- 1-inch ginger, peeled and minced
- ½ teaspoon of each ground cumin garam masala, paprika
- 1 teaspoon of ground coriander
- 15 ounces of can tomatoes or 2 large tomatoes, diced
- 1.5 cups of water
- ¾ teaspoon of salt
- 2-3 packed cups of chopped spinach chard or combination greens (10 to 12 ounces)
- 1 cup of non-dairy milk, thicker milks such as coconut milk or cashew milk or soy milk, or use almond milk blended with 2-3 tablespoons of cashews
- 1 tablespoon of lemon juice
- Cayenne and garam masala, for garnish

Cooking Instructions:

1. Soak the chickpeas in a cold water and wash well. Drain the soaked chickpeas and set aside.

2. Press the Sauté button and allow the Instant Pot to be hot for about 2 minutes.

3. Add the oil and spread using a spatula. In a medium bowl, mince and mix together the onion, ginger, garlic and hot chili.

4. Add the mixture to the hot oil and cook for about 3 to 4 minutes, stirring frequently.

5. Add the spices such as cumin garam masala, paprika, coriander and mix in.

6. Add the tomatoes and bring the pot to a boil. Add the washed and drained chickpeas, salt and water into the pot.

7. Close and lock the lid in place and set the knob on sealing position.

8. Select Manual function and cook on High Pressure for about 30 minutes.

9. When the time is up, use a quick pressure release for about 10 minutes.

10. Press the Sauté function again and add in the greens and non-dairy milk.

11. Taste and adjust the seasoning with additional salt.

12. Cook for about 4 to 5 minutes. Add the cayenne and lemon juice and mix in.

13. Serve warm over rice or with roti or naan and enjoy.

Sweet Potato Lentil Curry

Preparation time: 15 minutes

Cook time: 35 minutes

Total time: 50 minutes

Servings: 4

Calories: 200 kcal

Ingredients:

- ¾ cup of lentils or a mix of brown/green lentils and mung beans, soaked for about 15 minutes in warm hot
- 1 teaspoon of oil, or water
- ½ onion, chopped
- 4 cloves of garlic, chopped
- A pinch of ginger, chopped
- ½ or 1 hot green chili, chopped
- ¼ teaspoon of turmeric
- ½ - 1 teaspoon of garam masala
- ½ teaspoon of ground cumin or ground coriander
- 15 ounces of tomatoes 2 tomatoes, chopped
- 1 cup (heaping) chopped eggplant
- 1 cup of cubed sweet potatoes
- ¾ teaspoon of salt
- 2 cups of water, 3 cups for saucepan
- A few handful of spinach
- Cayenne and lemon/lime to taste
- Pepper flakes, for garnish

Cooking Instructions:

1. Soak the lentils in warm water for at least 15 minutes.

2. Press the Sauté function and add the oil. Once hot, add the onion, garlic, ginger, chili and a pinch of salt.

3. Cook for about 2 to 3 minutes, stirring frequently. Add the spices and mix in.

4. Add the tomatoes and cook for about 4 to 5 minutes. Mash the larger pieces.

5. Add your veggies, salt, lentils and water and give everything a good mix.

6. Close and lock the lid in place and ensure that the steam valve is set to sealing position.

7. Select Manual function and cook at High Pressure for about 12 minutes. When the time is up, use a natural pressure release for about 10 minutes.

8. Fold in spinach, cayenne and lemon/lime. Allow it to sit for about 2 minutes.

9. You can adjust to your desired consistency by adding more water or non-dairy milk for creamier and mix in.

10. Taste and adjust the seasoning with salt, garam masala or curry powder if desired.

11. Serve with flatbread or rice/cooked grains or as a soup with crackers and enjoy.

Vegan Mashed Potatoes

Preparation time: 10 minutes

Cook time: 20 minutes

Total time: 30 minutes

Servings: 6

Calories: 98 kcal

Ingredients:

- 5-6 potatoes, cubed into large pieces Yukon gold or baking potatoes, peeled
- 5 cloves of garlic
- ½ teaspoon of salt
- 1 tablespoon of extra virgin olive oil or vegan butter
- A dash of black pepper
- A dash of parsley or thyme
- A pinch of nutmeg
- 1 cup of full fat coconut milk
- Fresh chives, for garnish

Cooking Instructions:

1. Place the cubed potatoes, garlic cloves, ¼ teaspoon of salt with 1.5 cups water in the bottom of your Instant Pot.

2. Press the Manual function and set to cook at high pressure for about 4 minutes.

3. When the time is up, use a natural pressure release for about 5 minutes.

4. Place the potatoes into a large pot and pour enough water to cover them.

5. Bring the pot to a boil and simmer for about 10-15 mins, until they're fork-tender.

6. Transfer to a colander to drain them very well. Place the drained contents to a medium bowl and allow to sit for a couple of minutes to dry out.

7. Mash lightly and allow the steam to escape for some minutes and ensure to mash the cooked garlic.

8. Mix in salt, the remaining ingredients and half cup of coconut milk.

9. Mix and whip to add air and some texture. Allow to sit for a couple of minutes to enable the milk incorporate and absorb.

10. Taste and adjust the seasoning with ¼ teaspoon of salt. Add additional coconut milk for creamier consistency if desired and mix in.

11. Add 1 to 2 tablespoon of nutritional yeast if you desire cheesy potatoes.

12. Garnish with chives. Serve hot and enjoy.

Jackfruit Curry

Preparation time: 15 minutes

Cook time: 45 minutes

Total time: 1 hours

Servings: 2

Calories: 369 kcal

Ingredients:

- 1 teaspoon of oil
- ½ teaspoon of cumin seeds
- ½ teaspoon of mustard seeds
- ½ teaspoon of nigella seeds
- 2 bay leaves
- 2 dried red chilies
- 1 small onion, chopped
- 5 cloves of garlic, chopped
- 1-inch ginger, chopped
- 1 tsp coriander powder
- ½ teaspoon of turmeric
- ¼ teaspoon of black pepper
- 2 medium tomatoes pureed or 1.5 cups puree
- 1 20 ounces of can green Jackfruit drained and rinsed
- ½ - ¾ teaspoon of salt or to taste
- 1 - 1.5 cups of water

Cooking Instructions:

1. Heat the oil in a skillet over medium heat.

2. Once hot, add the cumin, mustard and nigella seeds and allow them to sizzle for about 2 minutes.

3. Add the bay leaves, red chilies and cook for a couple of seconds. Add in the onion, garlic and ginger and a dash of salt to taste.

4. Cook the ingredients until translucent for about 5 - 6 minutes stirring occasionally.

5. Add the coriander, turmeric, black pepper and give everything a good mix. Add the pureed tomato, salt and Jackfruit.

6. Give everything a good mix again, cover and cook for about 15 minutes. Uncover the pot and cook for a couple of minutes to allow the tomato puree to thicken.

7. Shred the Jackfruit, add water, cover and cook for additional 15 minutes. Taste and adjust the salt and spice to suit your desired taste.

8. Lower the heat to medium low, cover again and cook for additional 10 minutes until your desired consistency is achieved.

9. Garnish with cilantro and serve immediately.

Pad Thai

Preparation time: 15 minutes

Cook time: 10 minutes

Total time: 25 minutes

Servings: 6

Calories: 597 kcal

Ingredients:

- 2 teaspoons of sesame seed oil
- 1 tablespoon of minced garlic
- 1 teaspoon of grated fresh ginger OR ½ teaspoon of dry ground ginger
- ½ large onion, sliced
- 1 Package extra firm tofu cut into cubes
- 1 egg
- 4 tablespoons of rice vinegar
- 4 tablespoons of amino or soy sauce
- 1/3 cup of honey
- 1 diced zucchini
- 2 carrots, peeled and cut into sticks
- 2 bell peppers, sliced red and green
- 1 package or rice noodles
- 2 cups of vegetable stock
- ¼ cup of chopped basil
- ½ teaspoon of crushed red pepper, optional
- Garnish with cilantro peanuts, and lime

Cooking Instructions:

1. Press the Sauté setting on your Instant Pot and add the sesame oil.
2. When hot, add the garlic, ginger, and onions to sauté for about 1 minute.
3. Mix in the tofu and set aside. Add the egg and scramble in the Instant Pot.
4. When the egg is scrambled, mix together the egg with the tofu and onions.
5. Then, mix in the rice vinegar, amino, and honey.
6. Add the zucchini, bell peppers, and carrots.

7. Add the rice noodles whole in the bottom of your Instant Pot and pour the stock over the noodles.

8. Close and lock the lid in place and ensure that the valve is turned to sealing position.

9. Select the Manual function to cook on High Pressure for about 3 minutes.

10. When the time is up, use a natural pressure release and mix in the basil and red peppers.

11. Serve warm and garnish with cilantro, peanuts, and lime if needed.

CHAPTER: 10 SIDE DISHES

Rhubarb-Strawberry Compote with Fresh Mint

Preparation time: 10 minutes

Cook time: 10 minutes

Total time: 20 minutes

Serves: 4 cups

Ingredients:

- 2 lb. rhubarb, about 8 stalks
- ⅓ cup of water
- 1 lb. of strawberries, kept at room temperature
- 3 tbsp. of honey
- Fresh mint, minced, for garnish

Cooking Instructions:

1. Use a paring knife to peel the rhubarb stalks.
2. Chop them into ½ inch pieces. Add the chopped rhubarb and water into the bottom of your Instant Pot.
3. Close and lock the lid in place. Press Manual, High Pressure and set to cook for about 10 minutes.
4. Stem and quarter strawberries and set aside at room temperature.
5. When the time is up, use a natural pressure release before opening the lid. Add the strawberries and honey.
6. Give everything a good stir. Close and lock the lid in place.
7. Allow the strawberries simmer in hot rhubarb until soft for about 20 minutes.
8. Serve hot or cold with a garnish of fresh mint and enjoy!

Mac & Cheese

Ingredients:

- 2 cups of uncooked macaroni
- 2 cups of water
- ½ cup of evaporated milk
- 1 tablespoon of butter
- ½ teaspoon of salt
- 1 teaspoon of pepper
- ½ cup of shredded cheddar cheese
- ½ cup of shredded smoked gouda cheese

Cooking Instructions:

1. First, combine together the macaroni and water in the bottom of your Instant Pot.

2. Press Manual High Pressure and set to cook for about 6-7 minutes.

3. Ensure that you stir the noodles/water well before cooking to break up any clumps of noodles that might form.

4. When the time is up, use a natural pressure release for about 10 minutes.

5. Carefully remove the lid and dump in your cheeses, evaporated milk, salt, and butter.

6. Give everything a good mix for about 2 minutes or until it reaches a thick/creamy consistency.

7. Sprinkle with pepper and serve immediately.

Swedish Meatball

Preparation time: 20 minutes

Cook time: 5 minutes

Total time: 25 minutes

Servings: 9 servings

Ingredients:

- 2 eggs, slightly beaten
- ¼ cup of ketchup
- ¾ cup of dry bread crumbs
- 2 tablespoons of dried parsley flakes
- 2 tablespoon of Worcestershire sauce
- 1 teaspoon of onion powder
- 1 teaspoon of garlic powder
- 1 teaspoon of pepper
- 1 teaspoon of salt
- ½ teaspoon of chili powder
- 1 lb. of lean ground beef
- 1 lb. of ground pork
- 1 cup of beef broth
- 1 (0.87 oz) envelope brown gravy mix
- ½ cup of sour cream

Cooking Instructions:

1. In a medium bowl, combine together the eggs, ketchup, bread crumbs, and parsley.

2. Add the Worcestershire, onion powder, garlic powder, pepper, salt and chili powder.

3. Then, crumble the meats over the mixture and use your hands to mix well. Pour the 1 cup of beef broth into the bottom of your Instant Pot.

4. Carefully shape the meat mixture into meatballs and add them to your Instant Pot.

5. Close and lock the lid in place. Ensure that the valve is set to sealing position.

6. Select Manual High Pressure and set to cook for about 5 minutes.

7. When the time is up, use a natural pressure release for about 10 minutes.

8. Carefully remove the lid and scoop the meatballs on to a platter and tent with foil.

9. Set the Instant Pot on sauté setting and whisk in the package of gravy mix.

10. Bring the contents to a boil and stir for about 2 minutes. Carefully remove the inner pot from your Instant Pot.

11. Set on the counter for a few minutes and stir in ½ cup of sour cream. Add the season to suit your desired taste.

12. Serve gravy over the top of meatballs and enjoy!

Thai Chicken Rice Bowl

Servings: 4

Calories: 343 kcal

Ingredients:

- 2 tbsp. of olive oil
- 4 chicken breasts, about 2 lbs.
- 1 cup of uncooked long-grain white rice
- 2 cups of broth
- 1 tbsp. of peanut butter, optional
- ½ cup of sweet chili Thai sauce
- 3 tbsp. of soy sauce
- ½ tbsp. of fish sauce
- ½ tbsp. of ginger, minced
- ½ tbsp. of tbsp. of garlic, minced
- 1 tsp. of lime juice
- 1 tsp. of Sriracha or hot sauce
- Cilantro, optional for garnish
- Shredded zucchini, optional for garnish
- Shredded carrots, optional for garnish
- Bean sprouts, optional for garnish
- Peanuts, optional for garnish

Cooking Instructions:

1. Press the sauté setting on your Instant Pot and pour the olive oil. Sear the chicken breasts for about 2 to 3 minutes on each side to seal in their juices.

2. Remove the chicken breast to a glass baking dish. Mix together the sweet chili Thai sauce, soy sauce, fish sauce, ginger, garlic, lime juice, sriracha and peanut butter.

3. Pour the sauce over the chicken breasts and give everything a good stir to combine. Add the rice into the bottom of your Instant Pot, add the chicken and sauce over top.

4. Add the broth, close and lock the lid in place. Press the Manual High Pressure and set to cook for about 10 minutes. When the time is up, use a natural pressure release for about 10 minutes.

5. Shred the chicken with two forks and then mix with the rice. Garnish with cilantro, shredded veggies and peanuts. Add extra soy sauce to taste and serve immediately.

Instant Pot Lasagna

Servings: 6

Calories: 509 kcal

Ingredients:

- 1 pound of ground turkey or beef thawed and broken into chunks
- 1 cup of cottage cheese or ricotta
- 1 cup of Italian cheese blend
- 1 - 28 ounce of can crushed tomatoes
- 1 tablespoon of oregano
- 3 cups of spinach leaves
- 1 tablespoon of thyme
- 1 tablespoon of parsley
- 1 teaspoon of black pepper
- 1 tablespoon of onion powder
- 1 tablespoon of garlic salt
- 6 whole wheat lasagna noodles, we used uncooked

Cooking Instructions:

1. In a medium bowl, mix together the Italian cheese and cottage cheese.

2. In another bowl, combine together the crushed tomatoes, thyme, parsley, pepper, onion powder, and garlic salt.

3. Add the sauce in a 7-inch spring form pan. Layer the noodles, cheese mix, sauce, uncooked ground turkey, and spinach.

4. Repeat the same procedure till the pan is full. Use two layers of noodles.

5. Top with the rest of the cheese and cover with aluminum foil.

6. Make a foil sling to remove the pan from the Instant Pot when done.

7. Add 3 cups of water to the pot and use the foil string to place the lasagna in spring pan into the Instant Pot on top of the trivet.

8. Select Manual High Pressure and set to cook for about 35 minutes.

9. When the time is up, use a natural pressure release.

10. Carefully open the lid and remove the lasagna from your Instant Pot using the sling as handles.

11. Remove the foil covering the lasagna and place under broiler to brown the cheese.

12. Top with fresh basil and serve.

Spicy Creamed Corn

Preparation time: 5 minutes

Cook time: 10 minutes

Total time: 15 minutes

Ingredients:

- 32 oz. corn canned, fresh or frozen
- 8 oz. cream cheese cubed
- 1 stick butter 1/2 cup, cubed
- ½ cup milk
- ½ cup heavy cream
- 1 tbsp. bacon grease
- 1-2 tsp. cayenne pepper
- 1/2 tsp. black pepper
- 1 tbsp. sugar
- 1 tsp. salt

Cooking Instructions:

1. Add all the ingredients into the bottom of your Instant Pot.

2. Secure the lid in place and ensure that the valve is in sealing position.

3. Set to pressure cook on LOW for 10 minutes.

4. When timer beeps, do a quick pressure release.

5. Carefully open the lid and give everything a good stir

6. Serve and enjoy!

Gobi Masala

Preparation time: 2 minutes

Cook time: 5 minutes

Total time: 7 minutes

Ingredients:

- 1 large cauliflower - cleaned & cut into florets or readymade florets bags
- 2 tablespoons of olive oil
- 1 large onion, finely chopped
- 1 teaspoon of grated ginger OR ½ teaspoon of ginger powder
- 1 cup of water, remove 2 tablespoons to make dry gobhi or use whole 1 cup to make it slightly thick
- 4 tablespoons of chopped cilantro, optional

Spices:

- ½ teaspoon of turmeric powder
- 1 teaspoon of cumin seeds
- 1 tablespoon of coriander powder
- 1 tablespoon of cumin powder
- ½ tsp. of garam masala
- ½ tsp. of chili powder

Cooking Instructions:

1. Set your Instant Pot to Sauté mode.

2. When hot, add the oil, cumin seeds and cook for 30 seconds. Add the onions and sauté for 1 minute.

3. Add all the spices and cook for 30 seconds. Add the cauliflower florets, and water.

4. Secure the lid in place and ensure that the valve is in sealing position. Select Manual, High Pressure for 3 minutes.

5. When the timer beeps, do a quick pressure release. Carefully open the lid and add the chopped cilantro.

6. Give everything a good mix with a fork. Transfer to serving bowl and garnish some more with cilantro on top.

7. Serve and enjoy!

Creamy Garlic Broccoli Mash

Preparation time: 5 minutes

Cook time: 5 minutes

Total time: 10 minutes

Serves: 4

Ingredients:

- 1 tbsp. of unsalted butter
- 2 large cloves garlic, crushed
- 2 medium heads broccoli (about 1 lb./450 g), chopped
- ½ cup (120 ml) water
- 8 oz. (115 g) cream cheese
- ¼ tsp. of salt
- ¼ tsp. of black pepper
- ¼ tsp. of crushed red pepper flakes (optional)

Cooking Instructions:

1. Press the "Sauté" function and allow to heat up for 2 minutes.

2. Add the butter, garlic and sauté for about 30 seconds, stirring constantly. Press "Cancel" function.

3. Add all remaining ingredients into the bottom of your Instant Pot. Secure the lid in place and ensure that the valve is in sealing position.

4. Select Manual, High Pressure for 1 minute. When the timer beeps, do a quick pressure release.

5. Mash the broccoli with a potato masher, or use an immersion blender. Add more salt and pepper to taste if desired.

6. Serve and enjoy!

Cilantro Lime Cauliflower Rice

Preparation time: 5 minutes

Cook time: 1 minute

Total time: 6 minutes

Ingredients:

- 1 head of cauliflower
- 2 tbsp. of extra virgin coconut oil
- Juice of 1 lime
- 4 sprigs of cilantro

Cooking Instructions:

1. Unwrap and wash your cauliflower. Chop the cauliflower into florets.

2. Add the florets into a silicone trivet and place into the bottom of your Instant Pot. Pour 1 cup of water into your pot.

3. Secure the lid in place and ensure that the valve is in sealing position. Select Manual, High Pressure for 1 minute.

4. When the timer beeps, do a quick pressure release. Carefully open the lid and removed the trivet that contains the cauliflower.

5. Drain the water and place the pot to the Instant Pot. Add extra virgin coconut oil in the pot. Press the Sauté function.

6. Mash the cauliflower with a potato masher or wooden spoon until it is a rice consistency.

7. Add the juice of 1 lime to the cauliflower. Give everything a good stir and allow to cook for 1 minute.

8. Remove cauliflower from heat and top with minced cilantro.

9. Serve and enjoy!

Potato Salad

Servings: 8

Ingredients:

- 6 medium russet potatoes, peeled and cubed
- 1 ½ cups of water
- 4 large eggs
- ¼ cup of finely chopped onion
- 1 cup of mayonnaise
- 2 tbsp. of finely chopped fresh parsley
- 1 tbsp. of dill pickle juice
- 1 tbsp. of mustard
- Salt and pepper to taste

Cooking Instructions:

1. Place the steamer basket in the bottom of your Instant Pot.

2. Add the water, potatoes, and the eggs.

3. Close and lock the lid in place. Select High Pressure and set to cook for about 4 minutes.

4. When the time is up, turn off the Instant Pot and do a quick pressure release.

5. Carefully open the lid and remove the steamer basket from the Instant Pot.

6. Place the eggs into ice cold water and allow to cool. In a medium bowl, combine together the onion, mayo, parsley, pickle juice, and mustard.

7. Add the cooked potatoes and mix the mayonnaise mixture into the potatoes.

8. Peel and dice the 3 cooled eggs and stir into the potato salad. Add salt and pepper to suit your desired taste.

9. Add more mayonnaise to achieve your desired consistency if needed.

10. Chill for about 1 hour before serving. Top with slices of the remaining hard-boiled egg.

11. Serve and enjoy.

Salmon with Chili-Lime Sauce

Preparation time: 10 minutes

Cook time: 5 minutes

Total time: 15 minutes

Servings: 2

Calories: 400 kcal

Ingredients:

For steaming salmon:

- 2 salmon fillets 5 oz. each
- 1 cup of water
- Sea salt to taste
- Freshly ground black pepper to taste

For chili-lime sauce:

- 1 jalapeno seeds removed and diced
- 1 lime juiced
- 2 cloves garlic minced
- 1 tbsp. of honey
- 1 tbsp. of olive oil
- 1 tbsp. of hot water
- 1 tbsp. of chopped fresh parsley
- ½ tsp. of paprika
- ½ tsp. of cumin

Cooking Instructions:

1. In a medium bowl, combine and mix together all the sauce ingredients and set aside. Add water into the bottom of your Instant Pot.

2. Place the salmon fillets on top of a steam rack inside the pot. Generously season the top of the salmon fillets with salt and pepper to taste.

3. Close and lock the lid in place. Press the Steam mode and set to cook at High Pressure for about 5 minutes.

4. When the time is up, use a quick pressure release for about 10 minutes. Remove the lid and place the salmon to a serving plate.

5. Drizzle with chili-lime sauce and serve immediately.

Summer Picnic Potato Salad

Preparation time: 10 minutes

Cook time: 4 minutes

Total time: 14 minutes

Servings: 6

Ingredients:

- 2 -2.5 lb. of russet potatoes, peeled/cubed
- 1 ½ cups of water
- 4-6 eggs

For Dressing:

- ¾ cup of mayonnaise
- 2 tbsp. of fresh flat leaf parsley, chopped
- 2 tbsp. of dill pickles, chopped
- 1 stalk fresh celery, chopped
- ¼ cup of scallions, chopped
- 1 tbsp. of yellow mustard
- 1 tbsp. of fresh dill weed, optional
- 2 tsp. of TOG house seasoning to taste
- 1 tsp. of dill pickle juice
- ½ tsp. of sea salt
- ½ - 1 tsp. of paprika, for garnishing

Cooking Instructions:

1. Put the raw potatoes in water and allow to soak in water for about 30 minutes.

2. Grease a loaf pan and crack in eggs.

3. Pour 1.5 cups of water to Instant Pot. Drain the potatoes and add into the steamer basket.

4. Place the steamer basket into the inner cooking pot and put the loaf pan on top of steamer basket.

5. Close and lock the lid in place. Cook on High Pressure for about 4 minutes. When the time is up, use a quick pressure release.

6. While the potatoes and eggs are cooking, mix together all the dressing ingredients and keep them aside.

7. In a medium bowl, place the potatoes and fold out the eggs onto baking rack.

8. Gently incorporate the dressing into potatoes. Put the baking rack over bowl of potatoes and push through grates.

9. Sprinkle with Paprika and cover the bowl.

10. Place in the refrigerator to chill or serve immediately.

CHAPTER 11: APPETIZERS

Jalapeno Hot Popper & Chicken Dip

Preparation time: 3 minutes

Cook time: 12 minutes

Total time: 15 minutes

Servings: 10

Calories: 267 kcal

Ingredients:

- 1 lb. of boneless chicken breast
- 1 ounce of cream cheese
- 3 Jalapenos, sliced
- 1 ounce of cheddar cheese
- ¾ cup of sour cream
- ½ cup of panko bread crumbs
- ½ cup of water

Cooking Instructions:

1. Add the chicken breast, sliced Jalapenos, cream cheese and water in the bottom of your Instant pot.
2. Select Manual function, to cook on High Pressure for about 12 minutes.
3. When the time is up, use a quick pressure release.
4. Carefully open the lid and shred the chicken.
5. Stir in the cheddar cheese and sour cream.
6. Add in a baking dish and top with the rest of the cheese and panko bread crumbs.
7. Place in the broiler for about 2 to 3 minutes.
8. Serve and enjoy!

Prosciutto-Wrapped Asparagus Canes

Preparation time: 5 minutes

Cook time: 7 minutes

Total time: 12 minutes

Ingredients:

- 1 pound (500g) of thick Asparagus
- 8 ounces (225g) of thinly sliced Prosciutto

Cooking Instructions:

1. Add about 2 cups of water in your pressure cooker and set aside.
2. Wrap the asparagus spears in prosciutto.
3. Lay the extra un-wrapped spears to form a single layer along the bottom of the steamer basket.
4. These will serve as another trivet for the prosciutto and will also help to prevent the prosciutto from sticking.
5. Lay the prosciutto-wrapped asparagus on top in a single layer.
6. Carefully place the basket inside your pressure cooker.
7. Close and lock the lid in place. Turn the heat up high and when the pan reaches pressure, lower the heat and count 2-3 minutes cooking time at High Pressure.
8. When time is up, use a natural pressure release for about 10 minutes.
9. Carefully open the lid and remove the steamer basket.
10. Place the asparagus on a serving plate.
11. Serve warm and enjoy.

White Queso Dip

Preparation time: 10 minutes

Cook time: 20 minutes

Total time: 30 minutes

Servings: 10

Ingredients:

- ¾ pound of White American cheese slices
- 1 cup of queso shredded cheese mix
- 1 tbsp. of butter
- 1 8 ounces of package cream cheese
- 1 tbsp. of garlic
- 1 can rotel
- 1 tbsp. of milk
- 1 tsp. of oregano
- 1 cup of water

Cooking Instructions:

1. Pour 1 cup of water in the bottom of your Instant Pot.
2. Use a tin foil to cover the bottom of your Instant Pot safe bowl.
3. Place on a trivet that has been placed on the bottom of your Instant Pot.
4. Add all of the ingredients and cover the top of bowl with tin foil.
5. Select Manual function to cook on High Pressure for 18 minutes.
6. When the time is up, use a quick pressure release.
7. Carefully open the lid and remove the tin foil.
8. Whisk the contents until smooth.
9. Serve and enjoy.

Easy Artichokes

Preparation time: 10 minutes

Cook time: 8 minutes

Total time: 18 minutes

Servings: 3

Calories: 245 kcal

Ingredients:

- 3 artichokes medium size
- ½ cup of sour cream
- 3 tablespoons of mayonnaise
- 1 teaspoon of garlic, minced
- ¾ teaspoon of salt
- 1 teaspoon of dill, we used dried in a jar
- 2 tablespoons of parmesan cheese grated/shredded
- 1 cup of water

Cooking Instructions:

1. Use a knife to cut off the tops of your artichokes.

2. Add the 1 cup of water into the bottom of your Instant Pot.

3. Then, open your Kitchen Deluxe extendable handle vegetable steamer, pull down little legs on bottom of steamer, and carefully place into the bottom of your Instant Pot.

4. Place 3 artichokes in the vegetable steamer. Slightly open the leaves and sprinkle with some salt.

5. Close and lock the lid in place. Select Manual function and set to cook on High Pressure for about 8 minutes.

6. When the time is up, use a quick pressure release. Carefully open the lid and sprinkle the top of artichokes with more salt and shredded parmesan cheese.

7. In a medium bowl, mix together all the remaining ingredients and serve on the side as the perfect artichoke dip.

8. Serve and enjoy!

Dr. Pepper Barbecue Meatballs

Preparation time: 10 minutes

Cook time: 15 minutes

Total time: 25 minutes

Servings: 10

Calories: 231 kcal

Ingredients:

- 1 bag of Farm Rich Meatballs
- 1 can Dr. Pepper
- 1 tablespoon of garlic, minced
- 1 cup of tomato puree
- ¼ teaspoon of salt
- 1 pinch of pepper
- 1 tablespoon of Worcestershire sauce
- 1 tablespoon of orange juice
- ¼ cup of brown sugar
- ½ tablespoon of Sriracha, optional
- 1 tablespoon of spicy mustard, optional
- ½ cup of onion minced, optional

Cooking Instructions:

1. In a medium bowl, add the can of Dr. Pepper.
2. Add the remaining ingredients into the bowl except for the frozen meatballs.
3. Whisk the mixture together until it is well combined.
4. Pour the Dr. Pepper barbecue sauce into the bottom of your pressure cooker or Instant Pot.
5. Pour the frozen Farm Rich meatballs on top and give everything a good stir to coat all the meatballs with sauce.
6. Select Manual, pressure and set low pressure for about 12 minutes. When the time is up, use a quick pressure release.
7. Carefully open the lid and allow to cool to enable the sauce to thicken.
8. Serve and enjoy!

Hawaiian Meatballs

Servings: 4

Ingredients:

- 1 package of cooked perfect sweet Italian meatballs
- 1 can pineapple chunks with juice
- 1 red pepper, chopped
- ¾ cup of brown sugar
- 1 tbsp. of soy sauce
- ¼ cup of red onion
- 1/3 cup of water

Cooking Instructions:

1. Add the all the ingredients in your Instant Pot except for corn starch.

2. Give everything a good stir.

3. Close and lock the lid in place and ensure that the steam valve is set in sealing position.

4. Select Manual function and set to High Pressure for about 5 minutes.

5. When the time is up, use a quick pressure release.

6. Carefully open the lid and whisk in 1 tablespoon of cornstarch until thickened.

7. Serve over rice and enjoy.

Buffalo Chicken Dip

Preparation time: 10 minutes

Cook time: 7 minutes

Total time: 17 minutes

Serves: 12

Ingredients:

- 2 chicken breasts, skinless and boneless
- ½ cup of buffalo chicken sauce
- ¼ cup of water
- 4 ounces of cream cheese, half a container
- 4 ounces of ranch or blue cheese dressing, optional
- 1 stalk celery, chopped, (optional)
- ½ - 1 cup of shredded cheese, (optional)
- Salt and pepper, to taste

Cooking Instructions:

1. Add the buffalo chicken sauce, water and chicken into the bottom of your Instant Pot.

2. Select Manual function and set to cook on High Pressure for about 7 minutes.

3. When the time is up, use a natural pressure release.

4. Carefully open the lid and shred the chicken using two forks.

5. Stir in the cheese and dressing, if desired.

6. Scoop the buffalo dip into your serving plate.

7. Serve with chips or veggies for dipping and enjoy.

Sweet BBQ Meatballs

Yield: 42

Ingredients:

- 1 bag (48 oz.) frozen fully cooked beef meatballs
- 18 oz. BBQ sauce, we used Masterpiece Original
- 18 oz. of grape jelly

Cooking Instructions:

1. Place 1 cup of water into your pressure cooking pot.
2. Place the steamer basket in the bottom of your pressure cooking pot and add the frozen meatballs.
3. Pressure cook at High Pressure for about 5 minutes.
4. When the time is up, use a quick pressure release.
5. Carefully open the lid and remove the steamer basket.
6. Remove the meatballs from the pressure cooking pot and discard the cooking water.
7. Add BBQ sauce and grape jelly to pot.
8. Press the Sauté setting and cook, stirring frequently until the jelly is melted and the sauce is smooth.
9. Add the heated meatballs and give everything a good stir to combine.
10. Press Keep warm setting until you are ready to serve.
11. Serve and enjoy.

CHAPTER 12: DESSERTS

Lemon Cream Pie

Ingredient:

- ¾ cup of sugar
- 3 teaspoons of cornstarch
- ¾ cup of water
- ½ cup of fresh lemon juice
- 2 egg yolks, beaten
- 4 ounces of cream cheese, softened and cubed
- 1 cup of real whipped cream, sweetened with ¼ cup of powdered sugar
- 1 baked 9-inches pie shell

Cooking Instructions:

1. In a saucepan, mix together the sugar, cornstarch and water.

2. Add the juice and yolks.

3. Cook over medium heat until it boils, stirring constantly using a wire whisk for about 1 minute to thicken.

4. Remove the saucepan from heat and stir in cream cheese until it has melted.

5. Allow it to cool to room temperature. Then, mix ½ cup of whipped cream into the lemon mixture and gently spoon into cooled pie shell.

6. Cover with a foil or waxed paper and chill for at least 6 hours in the refrigerator.

7. Serve immediately and top with the remaining whipped cream.

Apple Cider

Servings: 6

Ingredients:

- 10 apples, preferably a mixture - granny smith and a red variety
- Orange
- 2 cinnamon sticks
- 1 cup of brown sugar
- 2 teaspoons of cloves
- 1 teaspoon of cardamom, optional
- Water

Cooking Instructions:

1. First, quarter the apples and oranges.

2. Add the quartered apples and oranges in the inner pot of your pressure cooker.

3. Add the spices and enough water to cover. Carefully put the inner cooking pot in your pressure cooker.

4. Close and lock the lid on the cooker and set it to cook on high pressure for about 10 minutes.

5. When the time is up, use a quick pressure release.

6. Mash the fruit and close the lid on again and cook on high pressure for about 5 minutes.

7. When the time is up again, use a natural pressure release. Strain the mixture through a fine mesh sieve into a bowl and let to cool.

8. Serve with a cinnamon stick and sliced apples or oranges and enjoy.

Applesauce

Ingredients:

- 6-8 medium to large apples such as Granny Smith, Gala, McIntosh, Fuji
- 1 cup of water
- 1-2 drops of cinnamon essential oil
- 1 teaspoon of organic cinnamon, optional

Cooking Instructions:

1. First, cut the apples into 2-inch chunks.

2. Discard the core, stem and seeds. Add the apples in the bottom of your Instant Pot along with 1 cup of water.

3. Close and lock the lid in place and ensure that the steam valve is set to sealing position.

4. Select Manual function to cook on High Pressure for about 8 minutes.

5. When the time is up, use a quick pressure release.

6. Carefully remove the lid and remove any excess water.

7. Blend with an electric mixer or immersion blender to smooth out applesauce to your desired consistency.

8. Add 1-2 drops of cinnamon oil or cinnamon powder to taste.

9. Allow to cool or place in the refrigerator to chill.

Mini-Lemon Cheesecakes

Serves: 6

Ingredients:

Preparation time: 10 minutes

Cook time: 8 minutes

Total time: 18 minutes

Ingredients:

- 6 half pint mason jars
- 16 ounces of cream cheese, at room temperature
- ½ cup of sugar
- 1 teaspoon of flour
- ½ teaspoon of vanilla
- ¼ cup of sour cream, at room temperature
- 1 tablespoon of lemon juice
- Zest of 1 lemon
- 3 eggs, at room temp
- 1 jar lemon curd
- Raspberries, optional
- 1.5 cups of water

Cooking Instructions:

1. In a medium bowl, beat together the cream cheese, sugar, and flour until mixture is creamy with no lumps.

2. Beat in vanilla, sour cream, lemon juice, and lemon zest it has well mixed well.

3. Beat in one egg at a time until it has well mixed and avoid overbeating.

4. Fill each of the jar with ¼ cup of cheesecake batter and carefully place 1 tablespoon of lemon curd on top of batter.

5. Add another ¼ cup of cheesecake batter to each jar on top of the lemon curd and loosely cover each of the jar with a piece of foil.

6. Pour 1.5 cups of water to the Instant Pot and place the trivet on the bottom. Gently arrange 3 jars on top of the trivet.

7. Close and lock the lid in place and ensure that the steam valve is set to the sealing position.

8 Select Manual function to cook on High Pressure for about 8 minutes.

9 When the time is up, use a natural pressure release for about 15 minutes.

10 Carefully open the lid and remove the jars from pot.

11 Allow to cool at room temperature and store in the refrigerator until ready to serve.

12 Garnish with additional lemon curd and raspberries.

13 Serve and enjoy.

Pineapple Upside-Down Cake

Ingredients:

- 1 box of yellow cake mix
- 1 can of pineapple slices
- Brown sugar
- Butter

Cooking Instructions:

1. Prepare and mix the cake according to the manufactures instructions.
2. Butter the bottom of a 6" or 7" cake pan and sprinkle brown sugar over bottom of pan.
3. Add the pineapple slices in the pan.
4. Add enough batter to fill the pan and cover the pan with a piece of foil.
5. Place the trivet and 1.5 cups of water into the bottom of your Instant Pot.
6. Arrange the cake pan on top of the trivet.
7. Select Manual function to cook on High Pressure for about 18 minutes.
8. When the time is up, use a natural pressure release.
9. Carefully open the lid and remove the cake. Uncover the cake and place on a cooling rack for about 10 mins.
10. Once cooled, turn the cake onto a plate for serving.
11. Serve and enjoy.

Caramel Flan

Ingredients:

- 4 large eggs
- 1 can sweetened condensed milk
- 1 cup of regular or low-fat milk
- ¾ cup of water
- 1 teaspoon of vanilla
- A pinch of salt
- ½ cup of maple syrup

Cooking Instructions:

1. In a medium bowl, beat the eggs.

2. Add rest of the ingredients and mix well. Add a thin layer of maple syrup across the ramekins.

3. Add the egg mixture over the maple syrup layer until ramekins are slightly more than ¾ full and cover the tops with aluminum foil.

4. Pour 1 cup of water into the bottom of your Instant Pot and add the trivet.

5. Gently stack two layers of ramekins and ensure that it stays below the fill line.

6. Select Manual function to cook on High Pressure for about 9 minutes.

7. When the time is up, use a natural pressure release for about 10 minutes.

8. Carefully open the lid and remove the ramekins.

9. Allow to cool and serve immediately.

Rhubarb-Strawberry Compote with Fresh Mint

Preparation time: 10 minutes

Cook time: 10 minutes

Total time: 20 minutes

Serves: 4

Ingredients:

- 2 lbs. of rhubarb, about 8 stalks
- ⅓ cup of water
- 1 lb. of strawberries, at room temperature
- 3 tbsp. of honey
- Fresh mint, minced, for garnish

Cooking Instructions:

1. Use a paring knife to peel the rhubarb stalks, as you would celery.
2. Chop the peeled rhubarb into ½ inch pieces.
3. Add the chopped rhubarb and water into the bottom of your Instant Pot.
4. Close and lock the lid in place and ensure that the steam valve is set to sealing position.
5. Press Manual function and set to cook on High Pressure for about 10 minutes.
6. Stem and quarter the strawberries and keep aside at room temperature.
7. When the time is up, use a natural pressure release.
8. Carefully open the lid and add the strawberries and honey.
9. Give everything a good stir. Close the lid again and allow the strawberries to simmer in hot rhubarb until soft for about 20 minutes.
10. Serve warm with a garnish of fresh mint and enjoy!

Carrot Nut Bread

Ingredients:

- 1 ⅓ cup of sugar
- 1 ½ cup of cold water
- 1 cup of ground raisins
- 2 large carrots, grated
- 1 teaspoon of cinnamon
- ½ teaspoon of allspice
- ¼ teaspoon of nutmeg
- ¼ teaspoon of salt
- 2 tablespoons of butter
- 1 cup of chopped walnuts
- 2 cups of flour
- 2 teaspoons of soda

Cooking Instructions:

1. In a saucepan, add the sugar, water, raisins, carrots, spices, and butter.

2. Boil the contents slowly for about 10 minutes. Remove from the heat and allow to cool down.

3. Add the nuts, flour, salt, and soda to the saucepan. Give everything a good stir and pour into the prepared pan. Grease the pan and add the butter.

4. Line the bottom of the pan with parchment paper. Pour in batter and pour 1-2 cups of water into the Instant Pot liner.

5. Place the cake pan on trivet with a foil sling. Close and lock the lid in place and ensure that the steam valve is set to sealing position.

6. Select Manual function to cook on High Pressure for about 60 minutes.

7. When the time is up, use a natural pressure release for about 10 minutes. Carefully open the lid and check for doneness using a toothpick.

8. If the toothpick comes out clean, then it's done. Remove the pan from the Instant Pot liner.

9. Remove the bread from pan and place on a wire rack to cool. When the bread has cooled, wrap the bread and wait a day to enable the flavors to mellow.

10. Serve and enjoy.

Cocoa Apple Bundt Cake

Ingredients:

- 3 eggs
- 2 cups of sugar
- 1 cup of butter
- ½ cup of water
- 1 tsp. of vanilla
- 2½ cups of flour
- 2 tbsp. of cocoa powder
- 1 tsp. of baking soda
- 1 tsp. of cinnamon
- 1 tsp. of allspice
- 1 cup of chocolate chips
- 2 cups of grated apples
- 1 cup of chopped walnuts or pecans, optional
- 1 cup of raisins or dried cranberries, optional

Cooking Instructions:

1. Generously grease a 6 cups Bundt pan and coat with a little cocoa powder. In a medium bowl, cream together the eggs, sugar, butter, water, and vanilla.

2. In another bowl, mix together the flour, cocoa powder, baking soda, cinnamon and allspice. Add the dry mixture to the creamed mixture. Fold in chocolate chips, apples, nuts and fruit if desired. Add ½ the batter into prepared pan.

3. Gently tap the pan down on counter a couple of times to remove the air bubbles and ensure that the batter fills in all the grooves in the pan.

4. Lightly cover the pan with foil. Pour 1 cup of water and place the trivet into the bottom of your Instant Pot.

5. Use a foil sling to carefully lower the cake into the pot. Select Manual function to cook on High Pressure for about 35 minutes.

6. When the time is up, use a natural pressure release for about 10 minutes. Carefully open the lid and remove the cake from pot.

7. Place the cake on rack for about 10 minutes to cool. Turn the cake out onto a serving plate and dust with powdered sugar or frosting of your desired choice.

8. Serve and enjoy.

NY Cherry Cheesecake with Ricotta

Ingredients:

- 7" spring form pan
- 2 eggs
- 1 ounce of ricotta cheese
- 1 ounce of cream cheese
- ¼ cup of sour cream
- 1 can of cherry pie filling
- 1 tablespoon of vanilla

For the Crust:

- Oreos
- 2 tablespoons of butter

Cooking Instructions:

1. Crumble the Oreos in a food processor and add in melted butter.
2. Place it into the bottom of your spring form pan.
3. Using a mixer, mix together the eggs and cheeses. Fold in sour cream and Vanilla.
4. Add the mixture in the spring form pan and pour 1 cup of water into the bottom of your instant pot.
5. Carefully place the trivet inside pot and place the spring form pan on top using a piece of foil.
6. Select Manual function, to cook on High Pressure for about 40 minutes.
7. When the time is up, use a quick pressure release. Carefully open the lid and remove it from the pot.
8. Allow it to cool on a cooling rack for about 12 hours.
9. Top with Cherries and serve immediately.

Instant Pot Salsa

Ingredients:

- 12 cups of diced, peeled & seeded fresh tomatoes
- 2 medium green peppers chopped & diced
- 3 large yellow onions chopped & diced
- 1 cup of seeded & chopped jalapeno peppers (You can roast first for a milder flavor)
- 36 ounces cans of tomato paste
- ½ cup of vinegar
- 3 tablespoons of sugar
- 1 tablespoon of salt
- 2 tablespoons of garlic powder
- 3 tablespoons of cayenne pepper (use less for milder heat)
- 4 tablespoons of cilantro (optional)

Cooking Instructions:

1. Combine all the ingredients in your Instant Pot.

2. Select the Manual function, cook on High Pressure for about 30 minutes.

3. When the time is up, allow it to release pressure naturally.

4. After natural pressure release, allow to cool and can or freeze in airtight containers.

5. Serve and enjoy.

Sweet and Spicy Meatballs

Preparation time: 5 minutes

Cooking time: 25 minutes

Total time: 30 minutes

Ingredients:

- 16 ounces of cooked perfect meatballs
- 12 oz. of chili sauce
- 12 oz. of grape jelly
- ½ cup of water
- ½ tbsp. of crushed red pepper
- ½ tsp. of cayenne pepper

Garnish:

- Chopped green onions (optional)

Cooking Instructions:

1. Add 16 oz. of cooked perfect meatballs to the Instant Pot.

2. Combine chili sauce, grape jelly, water and spices in a medium bowl, give everything a good stir to combine.

3. Pour the mixture over cooked perfect meatballs and stir to cover. Secure the Lid, select the Manual function, to cook for about 10 minutes.

4. When the time is up, do a quick pressure release. Garnish with chopped green onions.

5. Serve and enjoy.

Hawaiian Meatballs

Serves: 3 to 4

Ingredients:

- 1 package of cooked perfect sweet italian meatballs
- 1 can of pineapple chunks with juice
- 1 red pepper, chopped
- ¾ cup of brown sugar
- 1 tbsp. of soy sauce
- ¼ cup of red onion
- 1/3 cup of water

Cooking Instructions:

1. Place all the ingredients (except for corn starch) in your Instant Pot and give everything a good stir.

2. Secure the Lid, select the Manual function, cook on High Pressure for about 5 minutes.

3. When the time is up, do a quick pressure release.

4. After the pressure release, select the Sauté function on your Instant Pot, whisk in 1 tbsp. of cornstarch until thickened.

5. Serve over rice and enjoy.

White Queso Dip

Preparation time: 10 minutes

Cooking time: 20 minutes

Total time: 30 minutes

Serves: 9 to 10

Ingredients:

- ¾ pound of white American cheese slices
- 1 cup of queso shredded cheese mix
- 1 tbsp. of butter
- 18 ounces package cream cheese
- 1 tbsp. of garlic
- 1 can Rotel
- 1 tbsp. of milk
- 1 tsp. of oregano
- 1 cup of water

Cooking Instructions:

1. Add 1 cup of water in the bottom of the Instant Pot.
2. Cover the bottom of the Instant Pot safe bowl with tin foil
3. Place on a steamer rack that has been placed on the bottom of the Instant Pot.
4. Add in all ingredients and cover the top of the bowl with tin foil.
5. Secure the Lid, select the Manual function, cook on High Pressure for about 18 minutes.
6. When the timer beeps, do a quick pressure release and remove Lid carefully.
7. Remove tin foil and whisk immediately until smooth.
8. Serve and enjoy.

Cheddar Bacon Ale Dip

Total time: 25 minutes

Preparation time: 15 minutes.

Cooking time: 10 minutes.

Ingredients:

- 18 oz. cream cheese, softened
- ¼ cup of sour cream
- 1-1/2 tbsp. of Dijon mustard
- 1 tsp. of garlic powder
- 1 cup of beer or nonalcoholic beer
- 1 lb. of bacon strips, cooked and crumbled
- 2 cups of shredded cheddar cheese
- ¼ cup of heavy whipping cream
- 1 green onion, thinly sliced
- Soft pretzel bites

Cooking Instructions:

1. In a Pressure Cooker, combine cream cheese, sour cream, mustard and garlic powder until smooth.

2. Stir in beer, add bacon, reserving 2 tbsp. Secure the Lid and ensure that the valve is on sealing position.

3. Select the Manual function, cook on High Pressure for about 5 minutes.

4. When the time is up, do a quick pressure release. Select the Sauté function, and adjust for normal heat.

5. Stir in cheese and heavy cream. Cook and stir until mixture has thickened, for about 3 to 4 minutes.

6. Transfer to serving dish. Sprinkle with onion and reserved bacon. Serve with pretzel bun bites.

7. Serve and enjoy.

Buffalo Chicken Dip

Preparation time: 5 minutes

Cooking time: 20 minutes

Total time: 25 minutes

Serves: 7 to 8

Ingredients:

- ¾ cup of cottage cheese
- ¾ cup of plain Greek yogurt
- 2/3 shredded cheddar cheese
- 2 pounds of frozen chicken breasts
- ¾ cup of Frank's hot sauce
- ½ teaspoon of garlic powder
- ½ teaspoon of onion powder
- ¼ teaspoon of black pepper
- ½ teaspoon of dried dill
- ½ teaspoon of dried parsley
- ½ teaspoon of salt
- Goat or feta cheese crumbles garnish
- Green onions garnish

Cooking Instructions:

1. Add in frozen chicken breast and 1 cup of water to your Instant Pot insert.

2. Secure the Lid, ensure that the valve is on sealing position. Select the Manual function, cook on High Pressure for about 12 minutes.

3. When the time is up, allow it to release pressure naturally. While the chicken is cooking prepare your sauce.

4. In a blender mix together the cottage cheese, Greek yogurt, and seasoning (garlic powder, onion powder, pepper, salt, dill, and parsley) until smooth for 1 to 2 minutes.

5. When the chicken is done cooling, drain the liquid and shred the chicken in the Instant Pot using a hand mixer.

6. Select the Sauté function on your Instant Pot, mix in the cheese, buffalo sauce, and blended sauce.

7. When the cheese is melts, transfer the dip to an oven safe serving dish. Sprinkle with goat cheese if desired and place in the broiler until the top is golden, for about 5 minutes.

8. Remove from the oven and let the dip rest for 5 to 10 minutes. Top with green onions if you like.

9. Serve with celery, carrots, whole wheat cracker and enjoy.

Crispy Chicken Wings

Preparation time: 10 minutes

Cooking time: 30 minutes

Total time: 40 minutes

Ingredients:

- 2 pounds of chicken wingettes
- 2 cups of wing sauce
- 1 cup of water

For serving:

- Ranch, blue cheese, celery, carrots

Cooking Instructions:

1. Place the wings in the bottom of your Instant Pot, add in water and 1 cup of sauce.
2. Close and lock the Lid in place, select the Manual function, cook for about 10 minutes.
3. When the time is up, do a quick pressure release. While the wings are cooking, prepare a sheet pan with aluminum foil, then place a wire rack on top, and spray with cooking spray.
4. Preheat your oven to broil, with the rack, 6 inches from the top. Use tongs to remove the wings to the prepared pan.
5. Broil for 5 minutes, flip them and broil for another 5 minutes more. Baste them with remaining 1 cup of sauce and broil for 3 to 5 more minutes.
6. baste again, halfway through, flip and repeat on the other side.
7. Serve with ranch, blue cheese, celery and carrots.
8. Serve and enjoy.

Stuffed Peppers

Preparation time: 15 minutes

Cooking time: 10 minutes

Total time: 25 minutes

Serves: 7 to 8

Ingredients:

- 8 bell peppers
- ½ pound of ground beef
- 2 cups of uncooked minute rice
- 2 cups of water to cook your minute rice
- 1 ½ cups spaghetti sauce
- 1/3 cup of onion diced
- 1 cup of mozzarella cheese shredded
- ½ teaspoon of garlic salt

Cooking Instructions:

1. Add a bit of olive oil and select the Sauté function on your Instant Pot.

2. Add the ground beef and onions. Make your minute rice on the stove. Cook until meat is cooked and onions soften.

3. Pour in your spaghetti sauce and rice, give everything a good stir. Turn off your Instant Pot and remove pot.

4. Transfer contents into a separate bowl and wash your pot. Return the pot into your Instant Pot and pour in 1 ½ cups of water.

5. Open your kitchen deluxe vegetable steamer basket and lower it into the Instant Pot.

6. Cut off the tops of the bell peppers and remove seeds inside. Place 4 bell peppers into your steamer basket so they fit snuggly.

7. Add a bit of mozzarella cheese into the inside, bottom, of each bell pepper. Spoon rice and ground beef mixture into peppers until each one is almost filled up.

8. Add another bit of mozzarella cheese on the top of each pepper on top of the rice mixture.

9. Secure the Lid, ensure that the valve is on sealing position. Select the Manual function, cook on High Pressure for about 10 minutes.

10. When the time is up, do a quick pressure release. Use central ring hook to lift vegetable steamer out of the Instant Pot.

11. Serve and enjoy.

Potato Corn Chowder

Preparation time: 10 minutes

Cooking time: 10 minutes

Total time: 20 minutes

Serves: 5 to 6

Ingredients:

- 6 red potatoes diced
- 4 ears corn (kernels removed from cob, about 2 cups, can use frozen or canned)
- ¼ onion diced
- 3 cups of vegetable broth can use water but this is better
- ¾ cup of cheddar cheese
- 3 cups half and half
- 2 tablespoons of corn starch a bit more depending on how thick you want it
- 3 tablespoons of butter
- Pinch of salt

Cooking Instructions:

1. Dice all the veggies, select the Sauté function on your Instant Pot. Add in butter until melted, add diced onions and cook until soft.

2. Add vegetable broth, diced potatoes, and corn removed from the cob. Then add pinch of salt.

3. Secure the Lid, ensure that the valve is on sealing position. Select the Manual function, cook on High Pressure for about 10 minutes.

4. When the time is up, do a quick pressure release and open the Lid carefully. Add a bit of water to your cornstarch in a cup to use as a thickener.

5. Add to the pot and stir. Select the Sauté function on your Instant Pot to allow mixture to boil.

6. Add half and half and cheese slowly, stir and serve when it has thickened a bit.

7. Serve and enjoy.

Apple Pie Steel Cut Oats

Preparation time: 5 minutes

Cooking time: 20 minutes

Total time: 25 minutes

Serves: 5 to 6

Ingredients:

- 1 cup of steel cut oats
- 1-2 apples diced
- 1 ½ teaspoons of cinnamon
- ½ teaspoon of salt
- ¼ teaspoon of nutmeg fresh grated
- 3 cups of water

Cooking Instructions:

1. Add in all the ingredients in your Instant Pot. Secure the Lid, ensure that the valve is on sealing position.

2. Select the Manual function, cook for about 5 minutes. When the time is up, allow it to release pressure naturally for about 10 minutes.

3. Then, do a quick pressure release to get rid of the remaining pressure. Stir and remove pot from Instant Pot housing.

4. Serve with your favorite toppings and enjoy.

Creamy Macaroni and Cheese

Preparation time: 6 minutes

Cooking time: 4 minutes

Total time: 10 minutes

Serves: 7 to 8

Ingredients:

- 1 pound of Pasta - (we use large elbow macaroni noodles)
- 4 cups of water
- 4 tablespoons of butter
- 2 teaspoons of kosher or sea salt
- ½ teaspoon of black pepper
- 1 cup of heavy cream
- 8 ounces of sharp cheddar cheese, shredded
- 8 ounces of Mexican or Colby jack blend cheese, shredded

Cooking Instructions:

1. Pour pasta, water, salt, pepper and butter into your Instant Pot and give everything a good stir.

2. Secure the Lid, ensure that the valve is on sealing position. Select the Manual function, cook on High Pressure for about 4 minutes.

3. When the time is up, do a quick pressure release. Pour in both cheeses and cream and give everything a good stir.

4. Serve and enjoy.

Acknowledgement

In preparing the **"Instant Pot Pressure Cooker Cookbook"**, I sincerely wish to acknowledge my indebtedness to my wife Mrs. Clara Michael for her support and the wholehearted cooperation and vast experience of my two colleagues - Mrs. Laura Ward and Mrs. Tasha Sanders.

Michael Francis

www.ingramcontent.com/pod-product-compliance
Lightning Source LLC
Chambersburg PA
CBHW081741100526
44592CB00015B/2255